Mel Bay Presents

YOU CAN TEACH YOURSELF®

BLUES HARP

By Phil Duncan

You Can Teach Yourself Blues Harp is a unique blues harp method designed to help you learn today's music. Upon completion of this method, the student should have the confidence to handle the demands of most blues music. In addition, the student will develop the ability to hear and respond appropriately. The student will develop an appreciation for rhythm and blues through the harp.

CD CONTENTS*

This book is available either by itself or packaged with a companion audio and/or video recording. If you have purchased the book only, you may wish to purchase the recordings separately. The publisher strongly recommends using a recording along with the text to assure accuracy of interpretation and make learning easier and more enjoyable.

1 2 3 4 5 6

Visit us on the Web at www.melbay.com — E-mail us at email@melbay.com

Contents

To The Student:

The intention of this book is to start playing the sounds you like so that interest and enthusiasm are strengthened. This is done by developing materials that encourage your creativity, hoping that you are more likely to keep playing the harmonica, enjoy it more, and play it just for fun. So hang in there and keep on playing and having fun!

This book is also designed so that a beginner or intermediate student will gain the greatest results within the shortest amount of time. If you use any part of this book, you will increase your ability to play harmonica. Always start slowly and clearly, and gradually build speed for best results. **Practice, not luck,** pays off! Have fun and enjoy the harmonica.

Developing Success

There are three things that create musical growth and develop talent.

First: Listen to your favorite harp players.
Second: Always set a daily practice routine (i.e., number of repetitions or amount of time spent).
Third: Practice with a friend who plays guitar or keyboard, or use pre-recorded accompaniment cassettes. In other words, create a *"jam session"* with someone.

Practice Schedule

First Few Weeks
Fifteen to twenty minutes to help form the mouth position and strengthen the lip muscles. Form the lips to a single tone, blowing and drawing. Form the chords for rhythm playing. Practice the exercises for the chord rhythms.

Around the Fourth Week
Practice thirty to forty-five minutes each day on single tones and chord rhythms. Find a friend to "jam" with, or use the cassette with pre-recorded accompaniment.

Around the Eighth Week
Up to an hour a day, practicing riffs and licks, making up your own riffs, and "jamming" with your friends. Constantly review all the material. Begin to try "bending" a tone, making it go out of tune. Begin to record your playing and adjust your sound to suit your taste.

Around the Fourth Month
Continue to practice an hour each day. "Jam" using your own creative ideas, and begin to make them musical. (Recording yourself will help establish your own sound.) Continue to review the material in the book. Play, play, play.

Tip: It is always better to play something every day than nothing at all. Try to practice the same time every day. Make it a routine, but do it for love. The roughest time is the first six months on harmonica. After six months you have got it together. Congratulations! You will be on your way to a great deal of musical satisfaction through your achievements. Continue to enjoy and have fun.

Care And Cleaning

We will be using the 10-hole diatonic harmonica in the key of "C." The "plastic" or urethane-bodied harmonicas are recommended because they are impervious to moisture. The wooden-bodied harmonicas work well also, but the wood tends to swell. The wooden harmonicas are still favored by many players. Always have your dealer test your harmonica *before* you purchase it.

Keep your harmonica clean by wiping if off with a soft cotton cloth. Rinse the harmonica under the faucet, removing it quickly from the stream and shaking the excess water out of the harmonica by tapping it on the towel-covered hand. Store it in its original package or case.

The 10-Hole Harp

There are seven different tones or notes: A, B, C, D, E, F, and G. These notes are repeated over and over for the entire length of the harmonica.

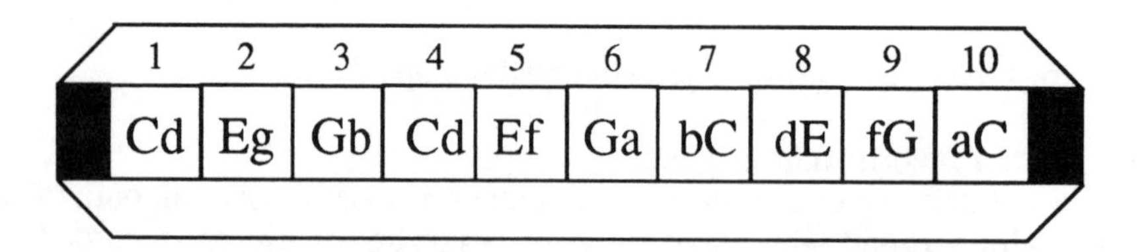

Let's begin with the 10-hole harmonica. The numbers should be along the top of the harmonica. Number 1 is on the left. Make sure the lowest tone is in hole 1 and the highest tone is in hole 10. If it is not, the covers are on upside down. Remove the covers and put them back on with the numbers on top and the lowest tone in hole 1. This is a very rare occurrence, but it is possible.

How To Read Arrows And Numbers

(1) Length of arrow is for duration of sound: 6 Long 6 Short

(2) An arrow pointing up means: BLOW

(3) An arrow pointing down means: DRAW (suck)

(4) The number tells which hole to Blow or Draw through.

Sixth hole:

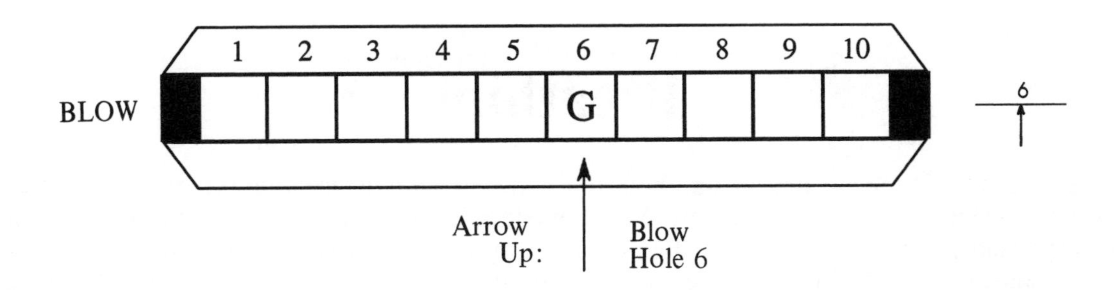

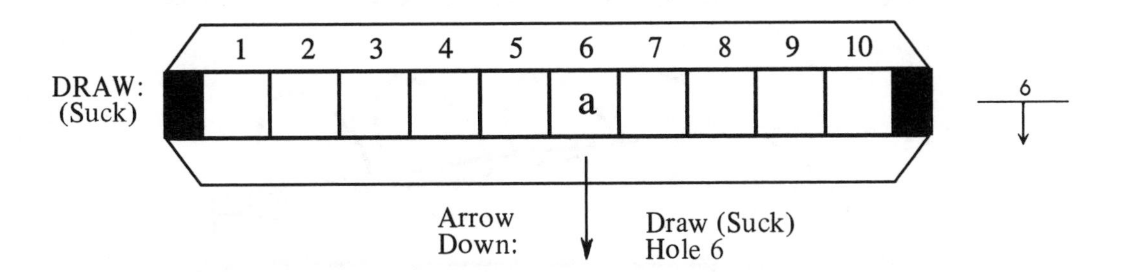

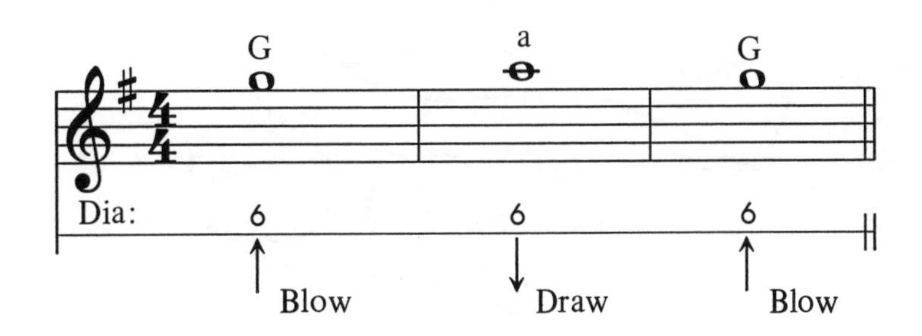

Air Flow

Projecting air in and out of the mouth is the way to make the harmonica work.

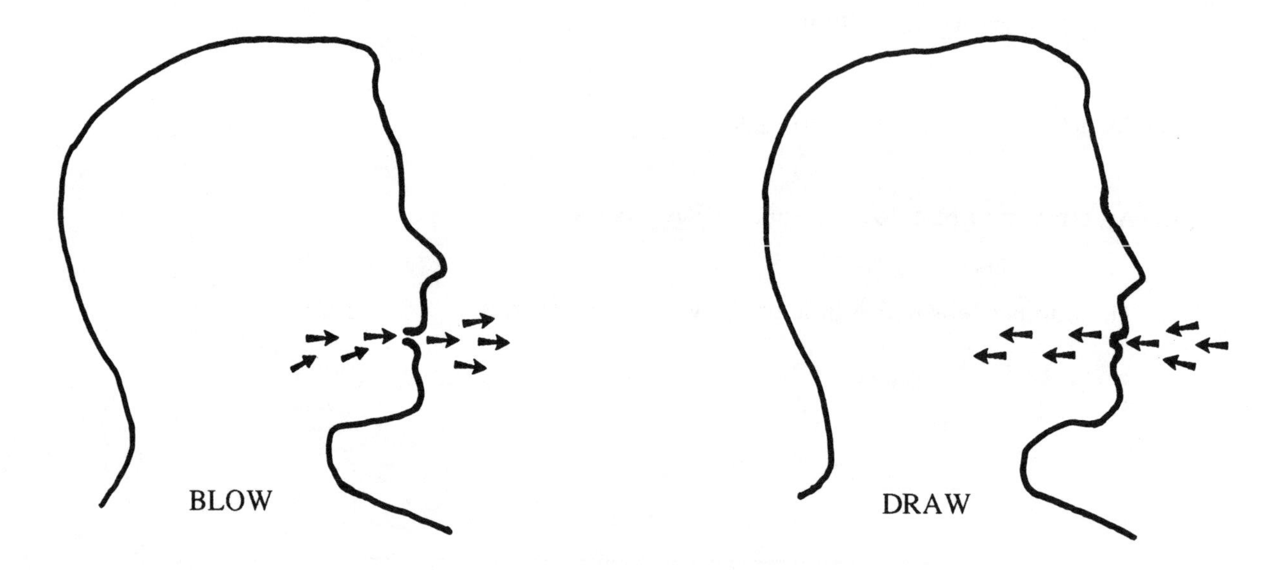

Breathing

Use the nose to help release air pressure. You do not have to remove the harmonica from your mouth to exhale excess air. Use your nose to do this. When applying air to the harmonica, be gentle (somewhat like blowing a feather through the air). Draw lightly, also. If you overdo the air pressure thing, you will choke the reed and it will not respond. Beginners seem to have this problem. It does not take a lot of air pressure to make a harmonica sound.

How To Hold The Harmonica

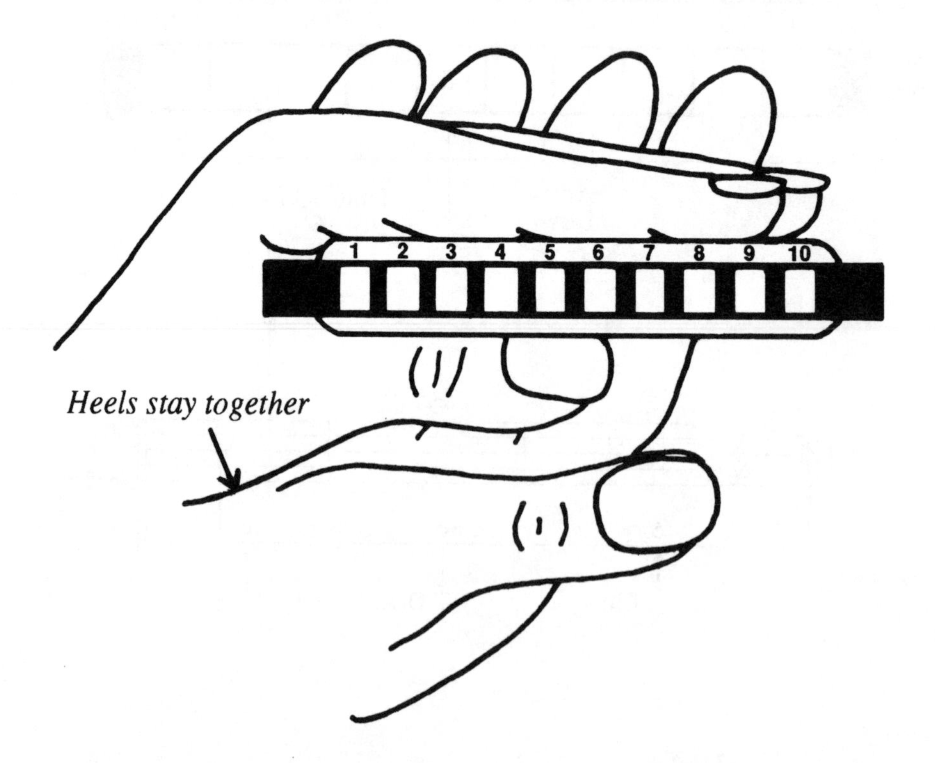

The 10-hole diatonic is held in the "V" of the left hand between the first finger and thumb. The right hand cups around the back of the harmonica.

Vibrato

Hand Vibrato

You may change the sound of your playing by adding a wavering tone, called *vibrato*. Holding the harmonica in the left hand, close and open the right hand over the left as shown above. This will create a wavering tone. As you move the right hand to and fro slowly, a rich mellow vibrato will result. By moving the right hand quickly, the wavering tones quicken. The heels of both hands stay in contact with each other, while the rest of the hand and fingers of the right hand move back and forth from close to open to close, etc.

Throat Or Diaphragm Vibrato

Using small puffs of air when exhaling into the harmonica will create a vibrato. While inhaling through the harmonica, reverse the puffs of air as you draw air through the harmonica. Do this in a slow four-count rhythm. Keep the puffs even. As you become familiar with this process, increase the number of puffs per long tone. Do this for blow and draw.

Amplification

If you are using the house amplification equipment, try to get a Shure 58 microphone. Separate microphones for singing and playing are preferred.

If you use an amplifier, the old tube type is usually the best. With the tube-type amplifier, use a Shure 520D or an Astatic JT30. A volume control on these microphones will help control feedback. Mic the amplifier through the house system by draping a house mic over the amplifier. Set the amplifier right next to you to avoid feedback. Have the return monitor set with lots of "presence" so that the sound will jump out at you and lift you up.

To set the house system, it should be warm in the middle (5, 6 out of a 10 setting), big on the bottom (lots of bass and depth, 7–9), and not too bright (1, 3 on the treble).

When it comes to equipment, bigger, louder, and more are not necessarily better. All amplification does is make your tone (sound) louder, not better. First and foremost is a good tone. Then you amplify that tone. It's not that amplification isn't good, just don't use it to create your sound. Always create and work on better tone without the amp, then apply that tone to amplification.

A good tone is produced in how you cup your hand around the harp and your embouchure (mouth, lips, and tongue position). Even the capacity of your lungs, throat, and mouth will determine to some extent the resulting tone.

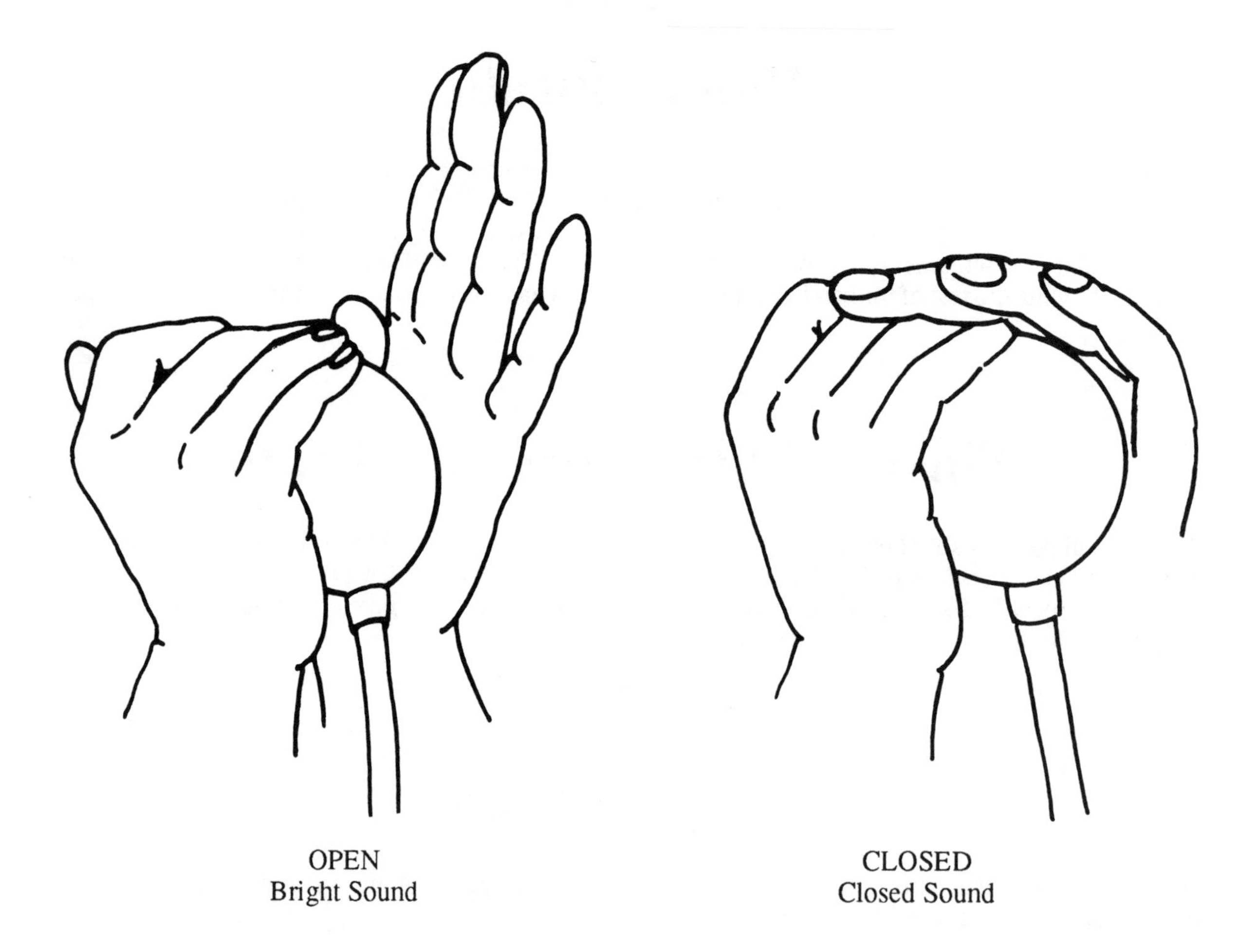

OPEN
Bright Sound

CLOSED
Closed Sound

Most music has four counts or beats to each measure. These beats must remain steady and even. It is suggested that a metronome be used to help control the steadiness of the beat. Tapping your foot can help, but the metronome forces the beat to be steady and even. This may seem monotonous, but it is necessary to establish a basis for syncopation and the ability to play along with other musicians.

Tip: Use a metronome to help keep a steady beat or rhythm. This will help you when you play along with other instruments.

Exact rhythm is necessary. It must be steady and even. Most people tap their feet to help keep the timing even and steady. Being able to play scales is a long-tried and tested method of developing smoothness of a flowing melody line. It is important to be able to play a line of music without hesitation.

Tap your foot for each count:

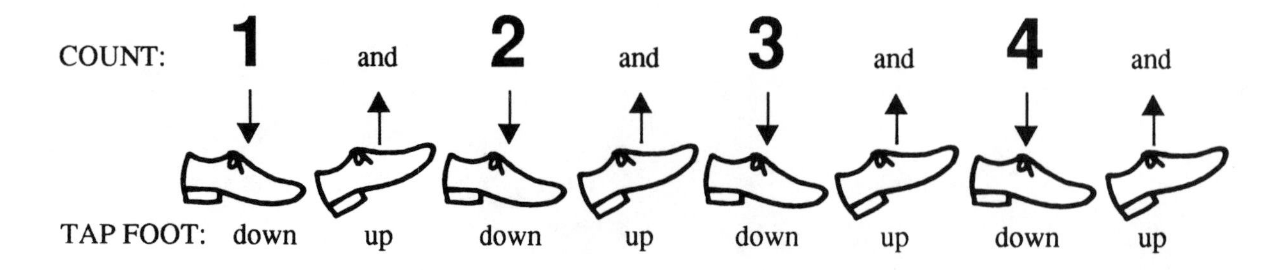

Even though we use a "C" harmonica, we use it in the key of "G." Below, the "G"s are highlighted. These tones are the "home" tones. These "G"s always "fit" the chord. This is called cross-harp in second position.

Cross-Harp

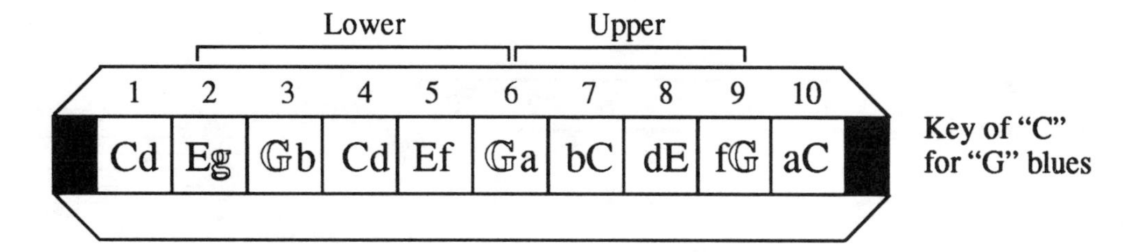

"C" harmonica uses the "G" scale for blues.

Most exercises will be notated in the key of "G" using the "C" diatonic harmonica. For the diatonic harmonica to change keys, just change harmonicas and read the same numbers.

C harmonica
G, A, B, C, D, E, F, G

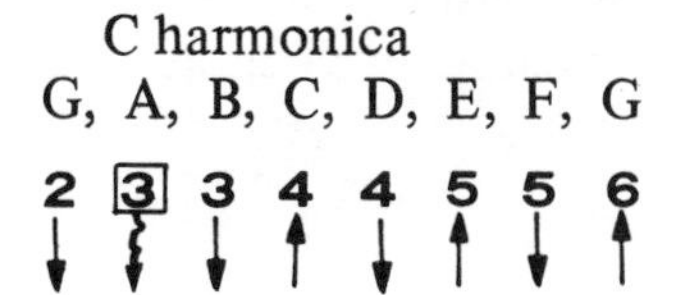

"Second position," "cross-harp," "blues harp," "blues harmonica," "Greek Mixolydian scale," and "dominant seventh scale" all refer to this kind of harmonica use. The real reason for this position (holes 2 through 6 and holes 6 through 9) is the flat seventh in the scale.

This is why the "G" scale on the "C" harmonica has a flat seventh tone. (The "C" scale has no sharps or flats.) Therefore, the seventh tone is "automatically" lowered to "F" natural, creating a flat seventh scale. Whatever the explanation, this scale sounds great with blues, country, and rock music.

Therefore the "C" harmonica plays in "G" blues. The following chart illustrates the cross-harp harmonica.

Actual Harp	Cross-Harp	Actual Harp	Cross-Harp
C harp	G blues	F harp	C blues
G harp	D blues	B♭ harp	F blues
D harp	A blues	E♭ harp	B♭ blues
A harp	E blues	A♭ harp	E♭ blues
E harp	B blues	D♭ harp	A♭ blues
B harp	F♯ G♭ blues	F♯ G♭ harp	D♭ blues

To play in any blues scale on the diatonic, just choose the harmonica that is four letters higher than the key in which the song is written. For example, with a guitar playing in the key of "A," the harmonica would be the "D" harmonica. If the guitar is playing in "G," the harmonica is "C." (See above examples.)

Chord Playing

(Rhythm)

A chord is three (3) or more tones played, BLOW or DRAW, at the same time.

Your mouth should be open enough to play three tones at the same time. Please lightly draw on holes 1, 2, and 3.

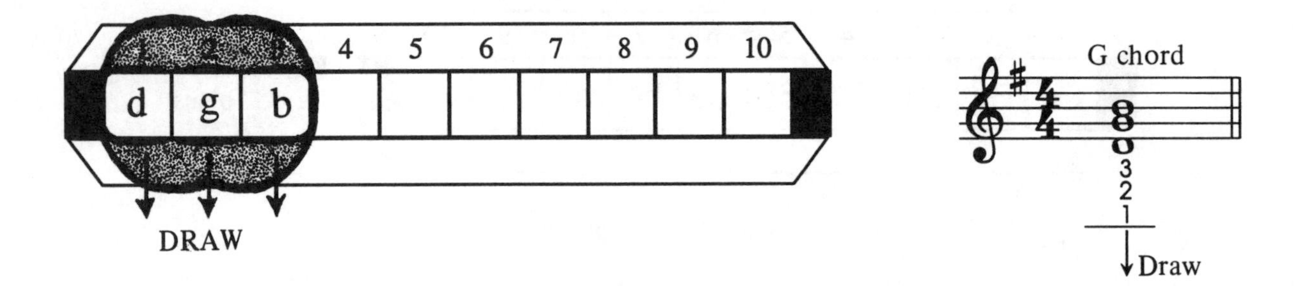

Play four draw chords in each section or measure. Make it sound a bit like a march. The dot ( ) under the chord means to "detach" or separate each chord. Do not connect one chord to the other. It should sound choppy and short!!! This is called staccato.

To experience the evenness before you play the harp say:

Then repeat that rhythm on the harp. There are four (4) quarter note chords in each measure.

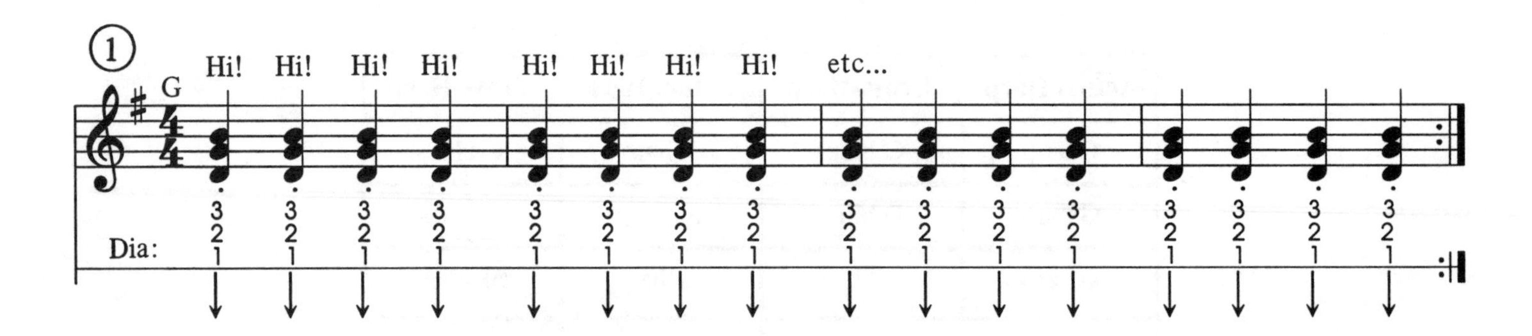

PLAY THIS 50 TIMES EACH DAY

Move your mouth to holes 2, 3, and 4. This time BLOW air gently through these holes. The sound should be a slightly higher pitch.

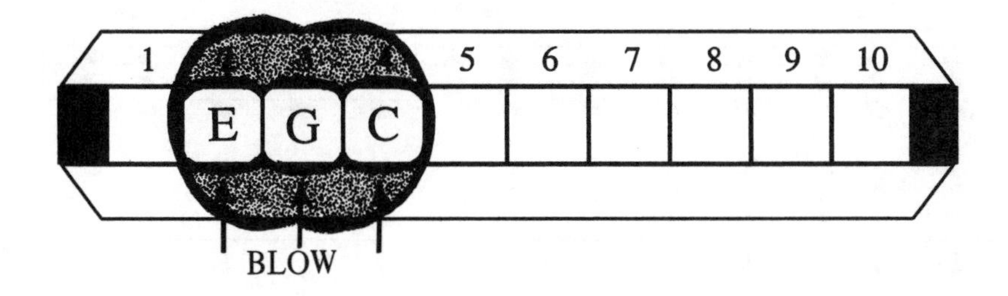

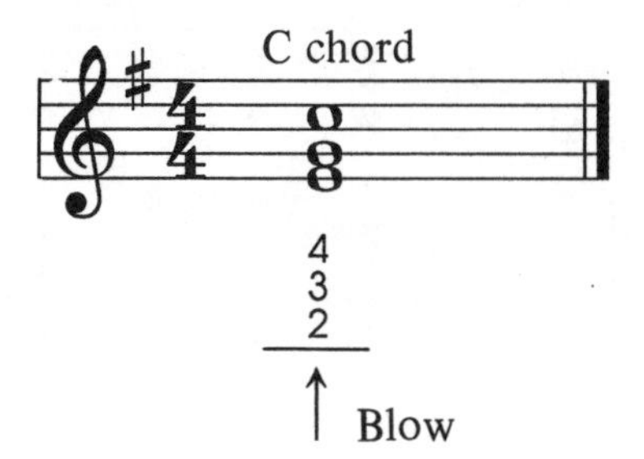

Notice the "C" chord is in holes 2, 3 and 4. But the draw (Suck) chord is on holes 1, 2 and 3. This causes the "G" chord to sound lower than the "C" chord. Remember to "Staccato" all chords. There are two sounds for the fourth count of each measure. This "C" chord uses "G" chord as a rhythm maker.

Being able to say the rhythm will enhance your grasp of the rhythm. Say "Hi!" for the quarter note chord and "Hil-ly" for the eighth note chords:

Repeat this pattern several times then play this rhythm on your harp using the correct holes.

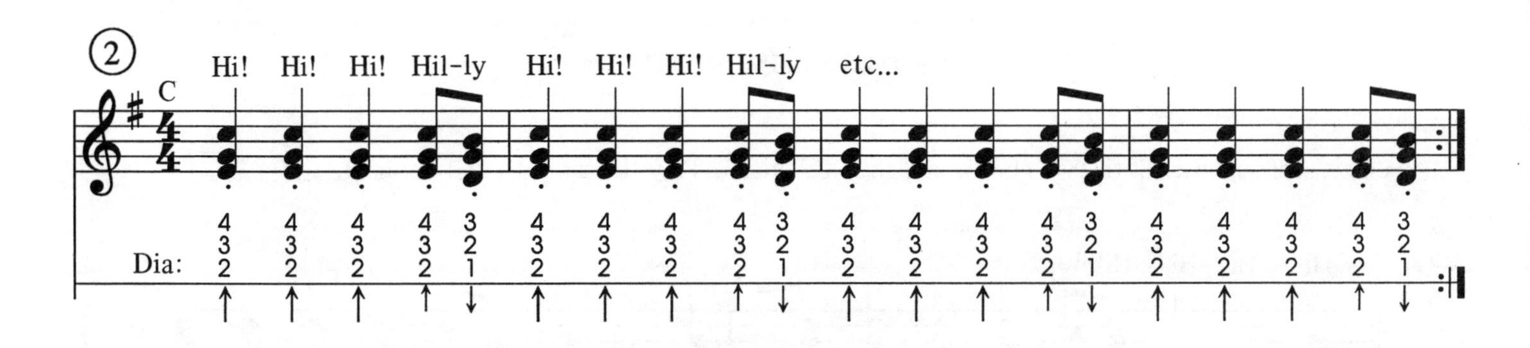

PLAY THIS 50 TIMES EACH DAY

The "G" chord will use the "C" chord as the rhythm maker.

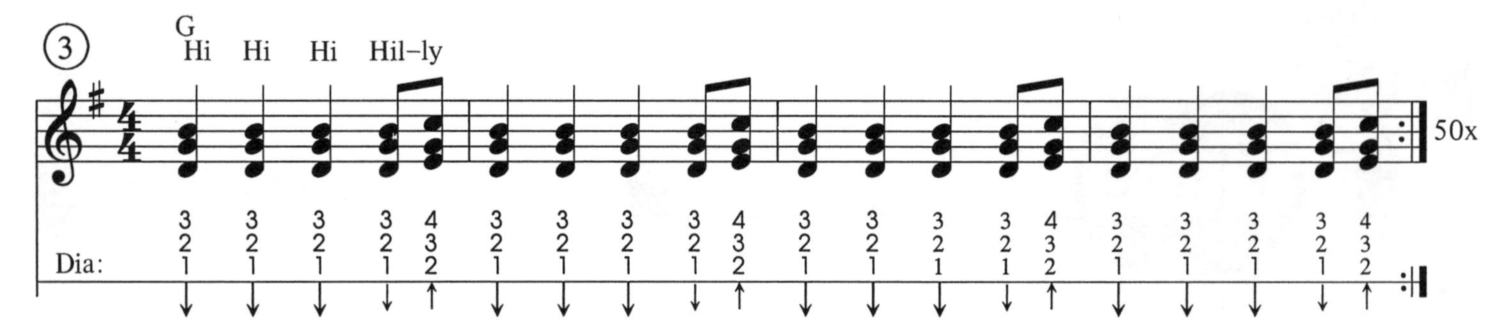

This next chord is also a "G" chord. It's a higher set of pitches than the last "G" chord or the last "C" chord.

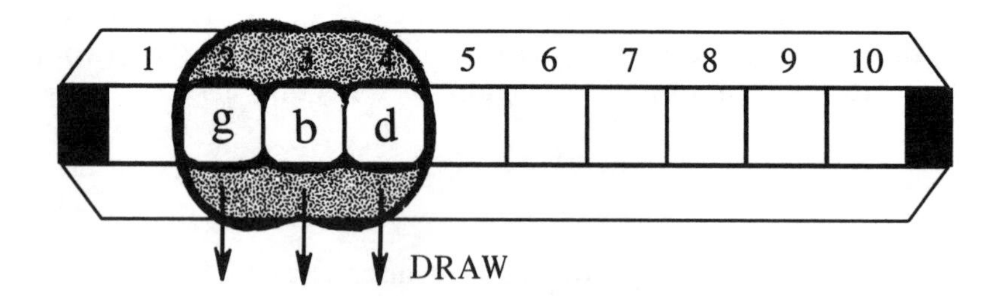

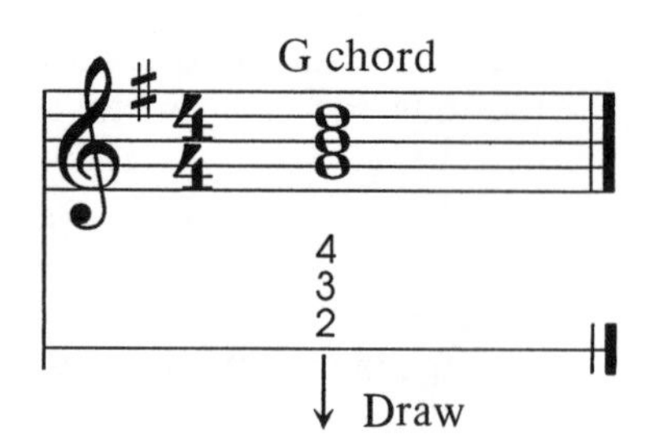

Notice the holes are 2, 3, and 4 are both draw and blow. You do not need to move the harmonica. You may play this smoother or legato, connecting each sound to the next.

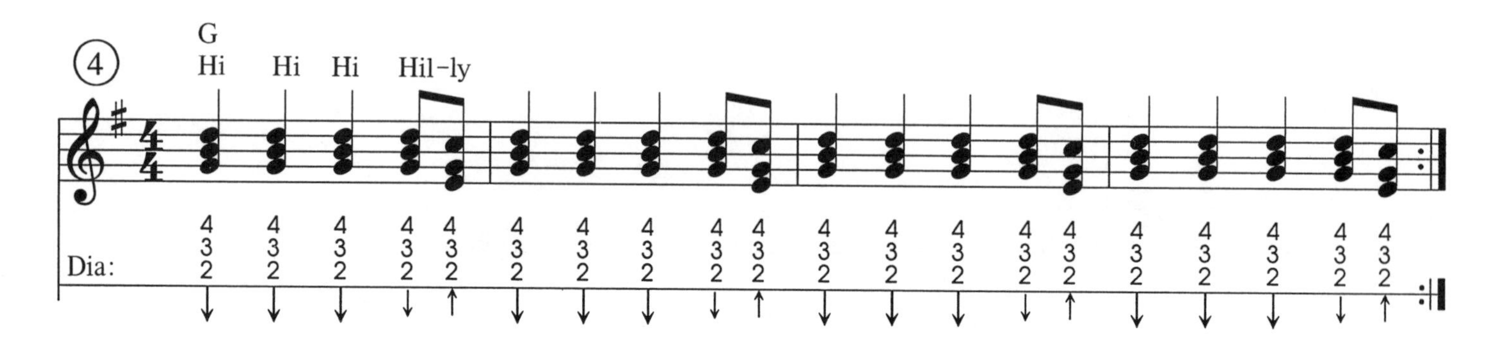

PLAY THIS 50 TIMES EACH DAY

This next segment uses both "G" chords and the "C" chord. Play this smooth and connected. (Legato)

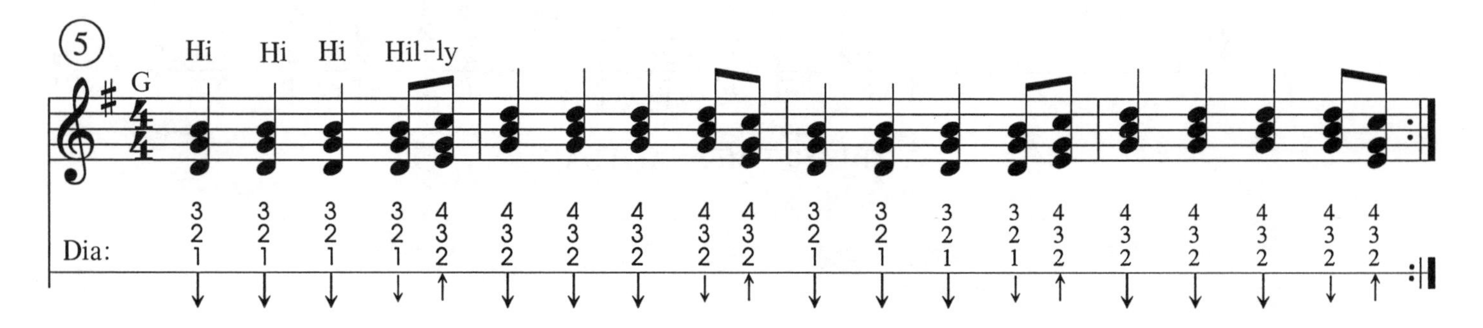

PLAY THIS 50 TIMES EACH DAY

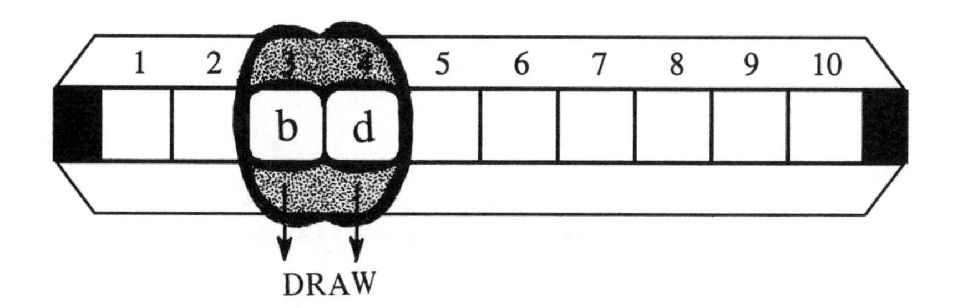

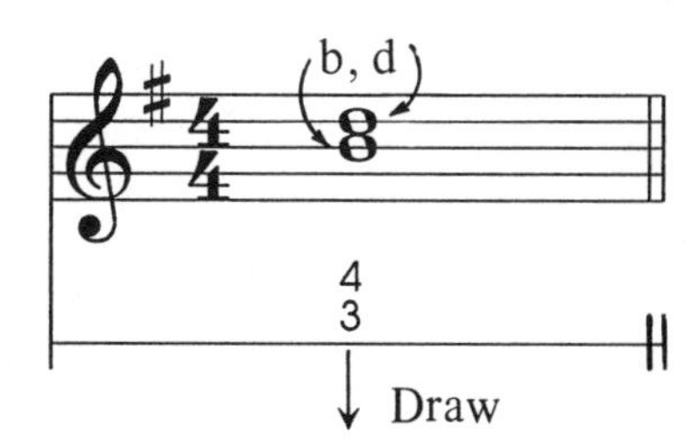

Most blues are played in a 12 measure form. Here is an example.

Bluzze

P. Duncan

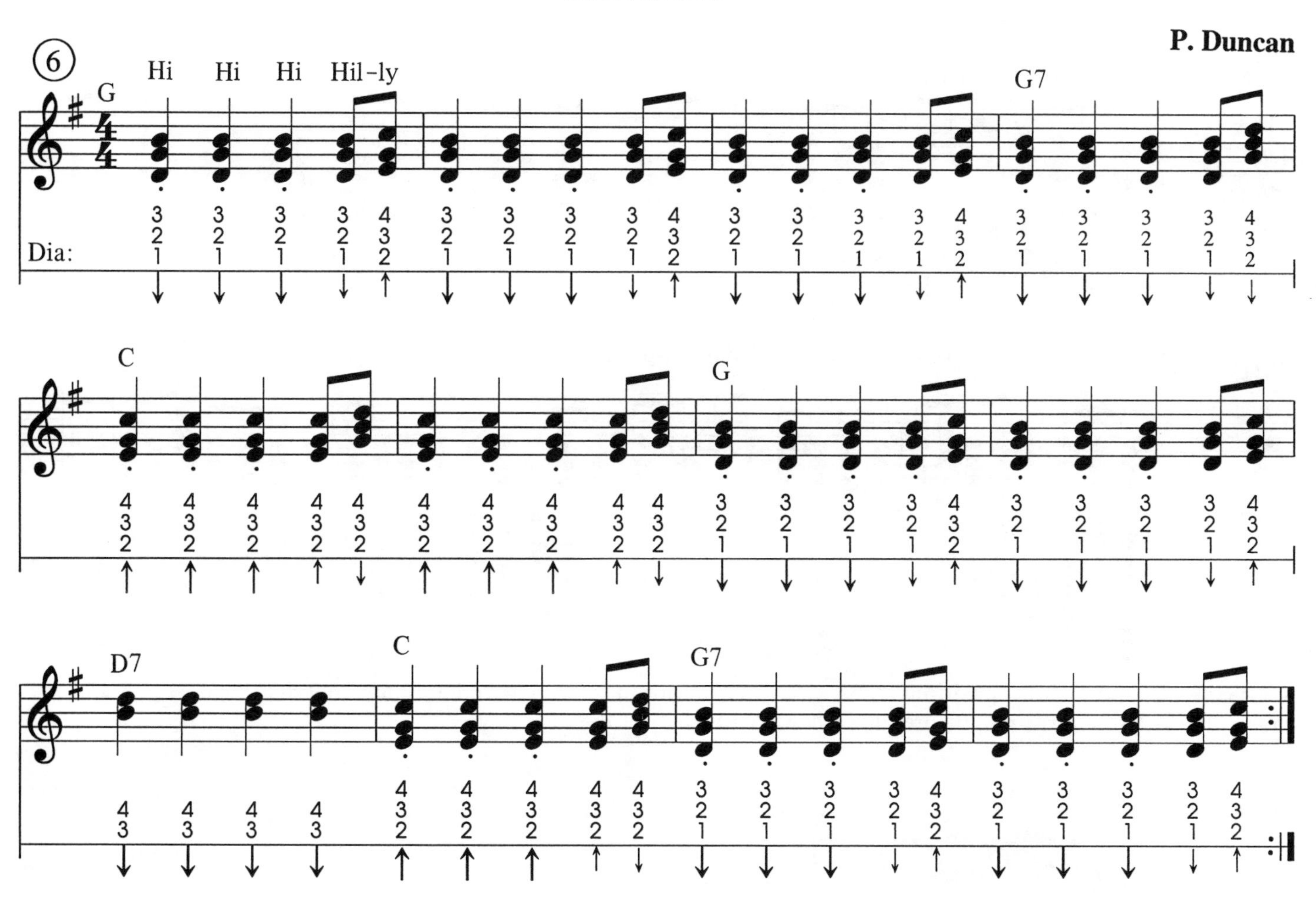

Let's double each chord, playing each chord twice. This can be played even or as a shuffle.

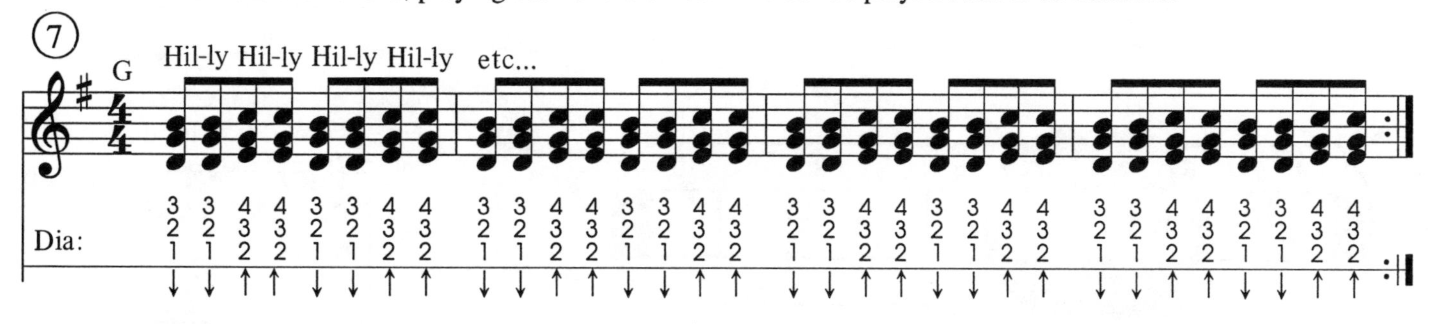

PLAY THIS 50 TIMES EACH DAY

This chord pattern changes in the second* and fourth* measures or sections. This can be played even or as a shuffle.

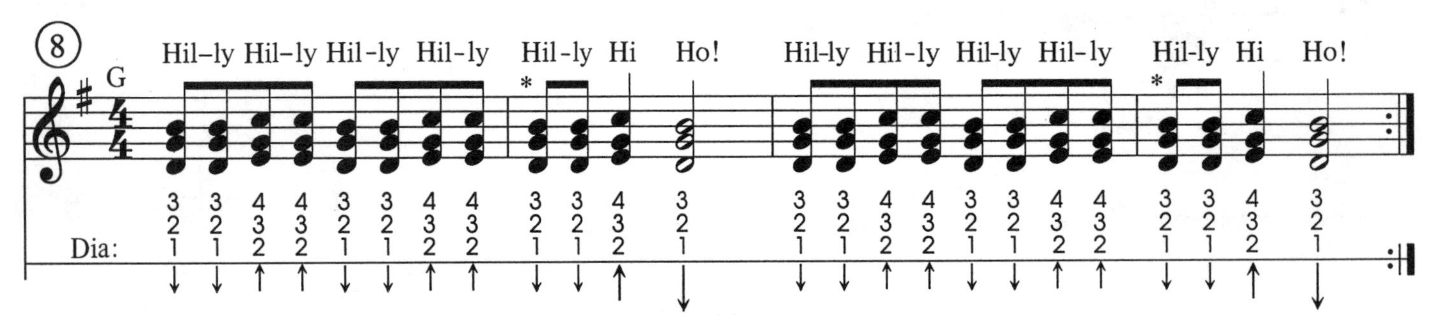

Here are two more patterns for chord rhythm playing.

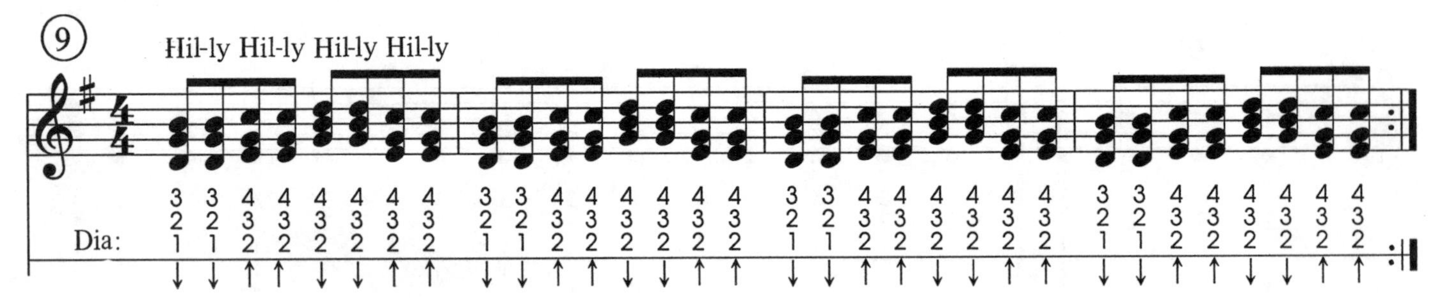

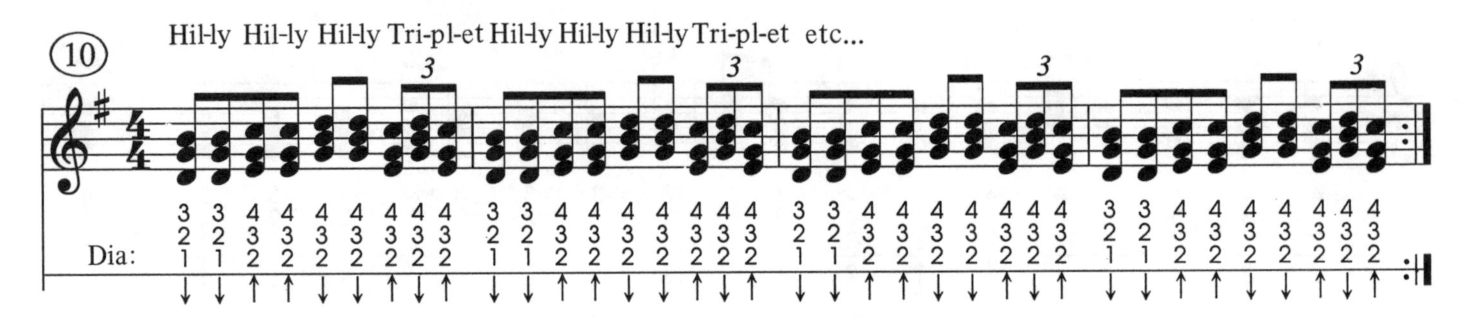

There are two more chord positions to be used. "C" chord in holes 3, 4 and 5, blow; and "G7" chord 3, 4 and 5, draw. These two chords will be used in "Chord-A-Mania" on the next page.

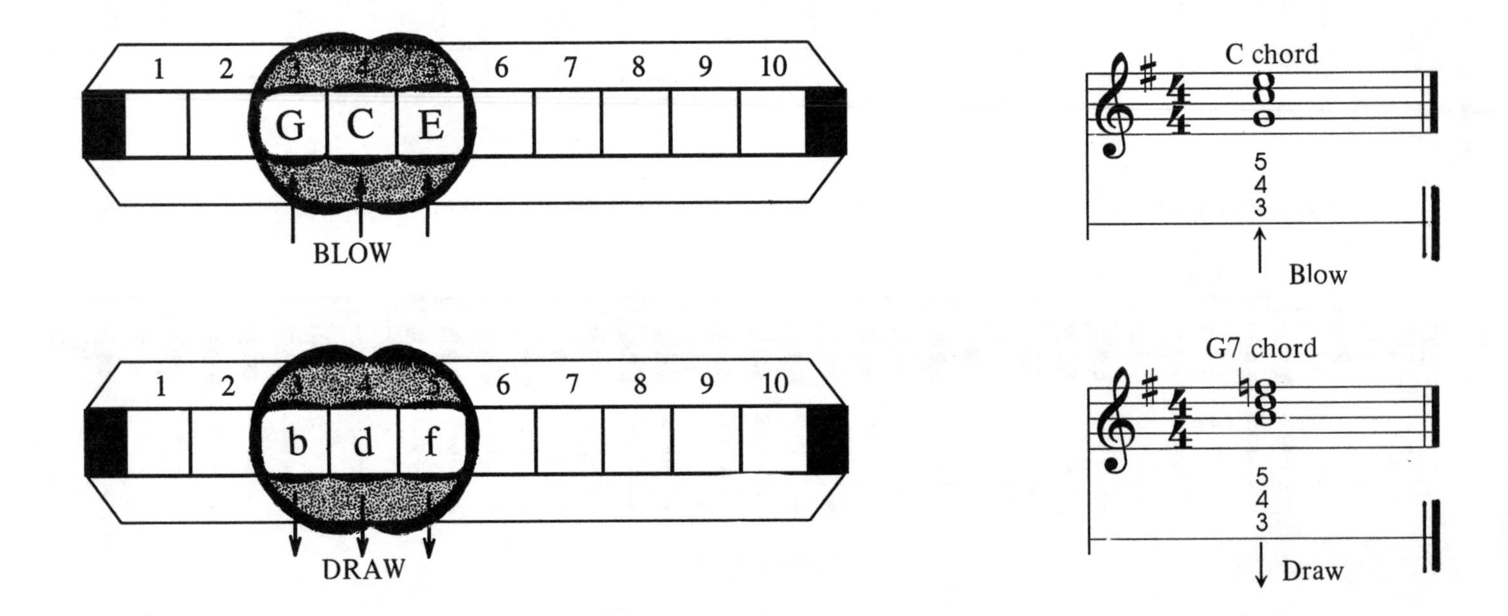

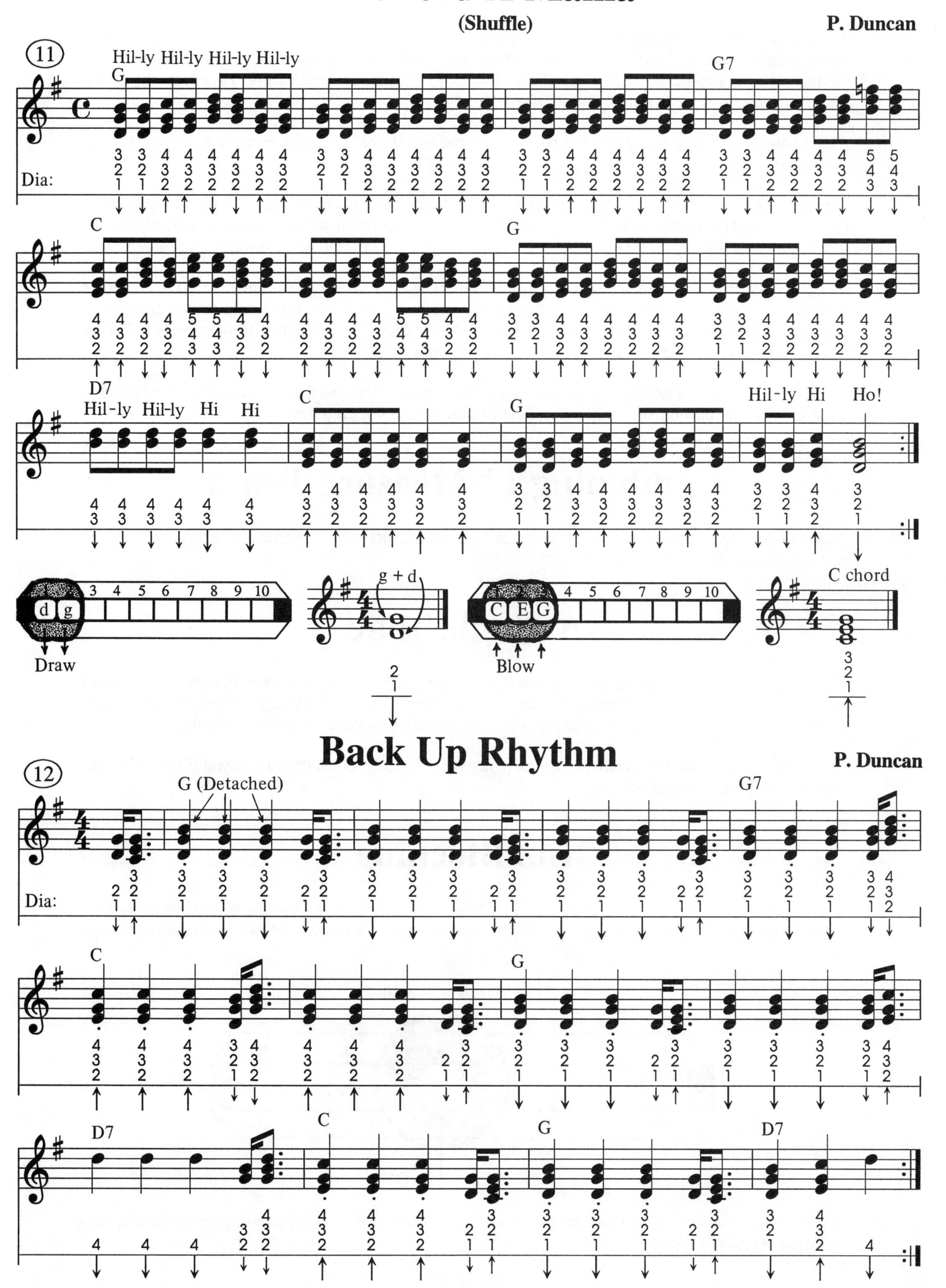

Chord-A-Mania
(Shuffle)
P. Duncan
11
Hil-ly Hil-ly Hil-ly Hil-ly
G
G7
Dia:
C
G
D7
Hil-ly Hil-ly Hi Hi
C
G
Hil-ly Hi Ho!
3 4 5 6 7 8 9 10
d g
Draw
g + d
C E G
4 5 6 7 8 9 10
Blow
C chord
Back Up Rhythm
P. Duncan
12
G (Detached)
G7
Dia:
C
G
D7
C
G
D7

Single Tone Section

The following section on single-tone development (no bends) will allow for accurate single-tone target. Some notation will be introduced, such as whole note, half note, quarter note, eighth note, and their equivalent rests (silence). These symbols are guides to enhance understanding. However, the arrow length also expresses duration or length of sound.

Each exercise will introduce a specific hole to be mastered. Work until each exercise is played without hesitation.

Most of these tunes can be played as a solo in a band. If you have a friend who plays guitar, "jam" with him or her to get the feeling of playing together. If a "garage" band (non-professional; just a practice band) is available, use these passages to join in. It is uncomfortable at first, but the reward is self-inspiring.

You will notice that some notes "clash" with the chord change. That is why sometimes we move to another hole or tone to make it "fit." However, there are exceptions, where the same note or passage can be repeated throughout the 12 measures. Most tunes (12 measures) are designed to be repeated. This is because the tunes can be used many times within the same song.

It is suggested that you rehearse each exercise or 12-bar tune at least 50 times each day until it becomes a natural part of your playing. Otherwise, at least play something each day.

Combining 12-Measure Tunes

These 12-bar blues patterns can be combined and played back to back for variety. Use any combination of tunes for 24, 36, 48, or more choruses.

A Single Tone

Pursing, puckering like sipping coffee or hot tea, whistling, and sucking a thick malt through a straw all describe the embouchure (mouth position on the harmonica) used for blues harp. Whatever helps you to position your lips for this style of playing will be necessary to succeed with this technique.

Sometimes this technique is called cross-harp, probably because blues harp is played differently than standard playing procedures.

Lip Blocking

This technique for playing is called *lip blocking*. The tongue is usually back in the mouth and the lips are pursed, that is, making the lips taller than wider, somewhat like a whistle or blowing or sucking through a straw.

Purse or pucker your lips

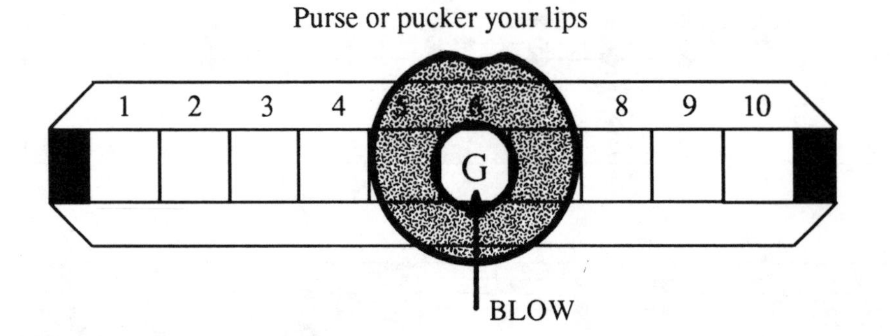

It may be necessary to move the harmonica to the right or left while you are creating an air stream, so as to target one single tone.

Single Tone Development
Vibrato

Use short puffs of air exhaling and inhaling to create a throat vibrato. On the "G" tone start slowly, four puffs on each tone, then speed up as this technique becomes comfortable.

A whole note equals four (4) beats or counts 𝅝 = 4

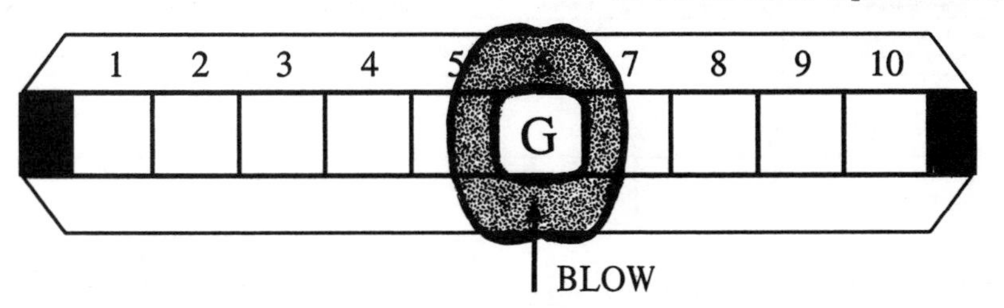

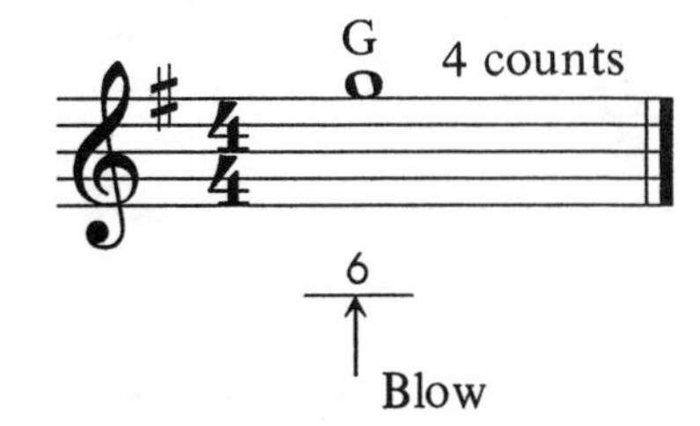

G Note Blues

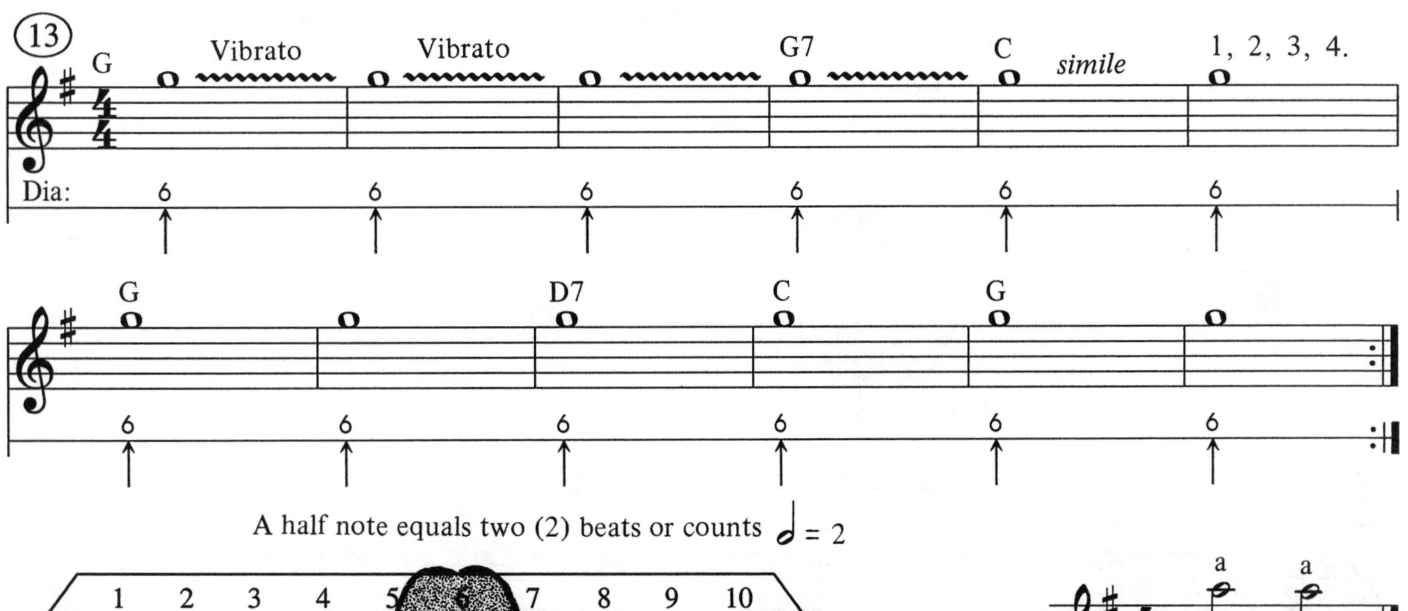

A half note equals two (2) beats or counts 𝅗𝅥 = 2

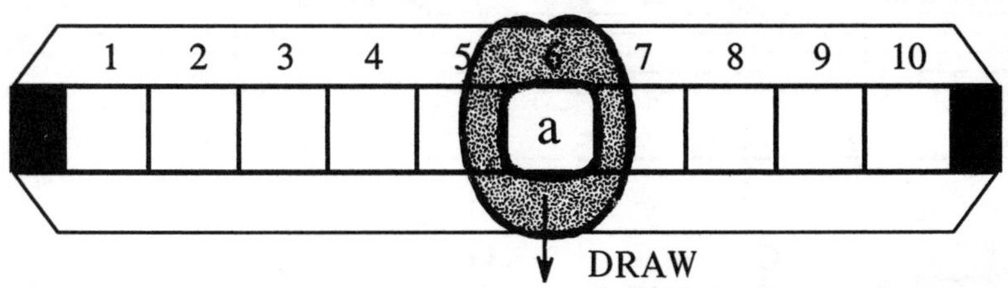

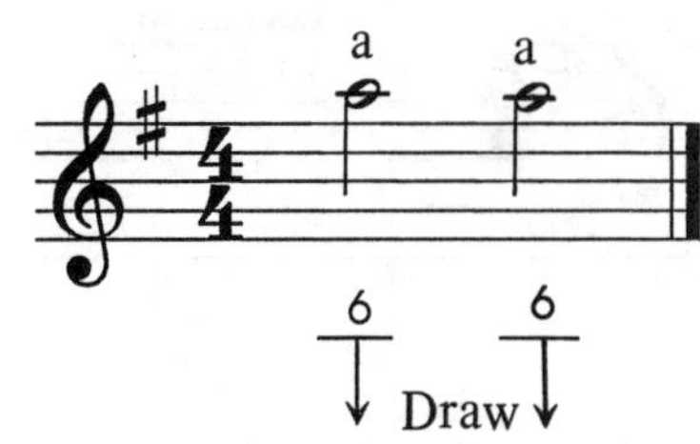

A Note Blues

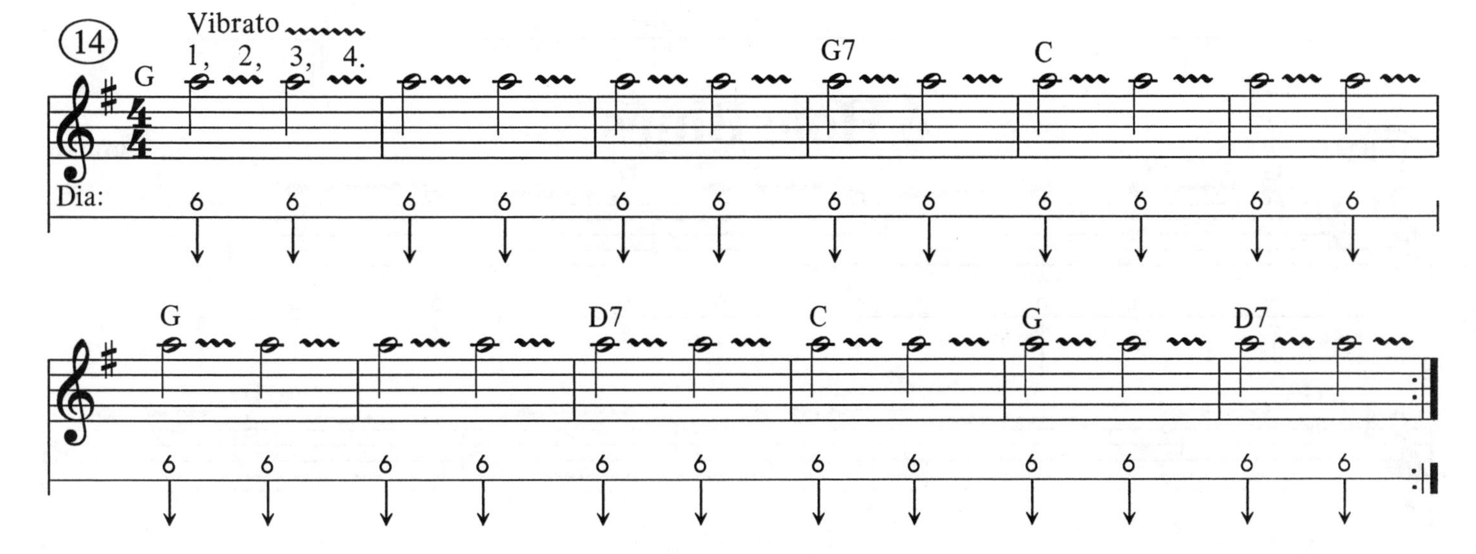

Some notes do not "fit." Here is a tune where each note "fits."

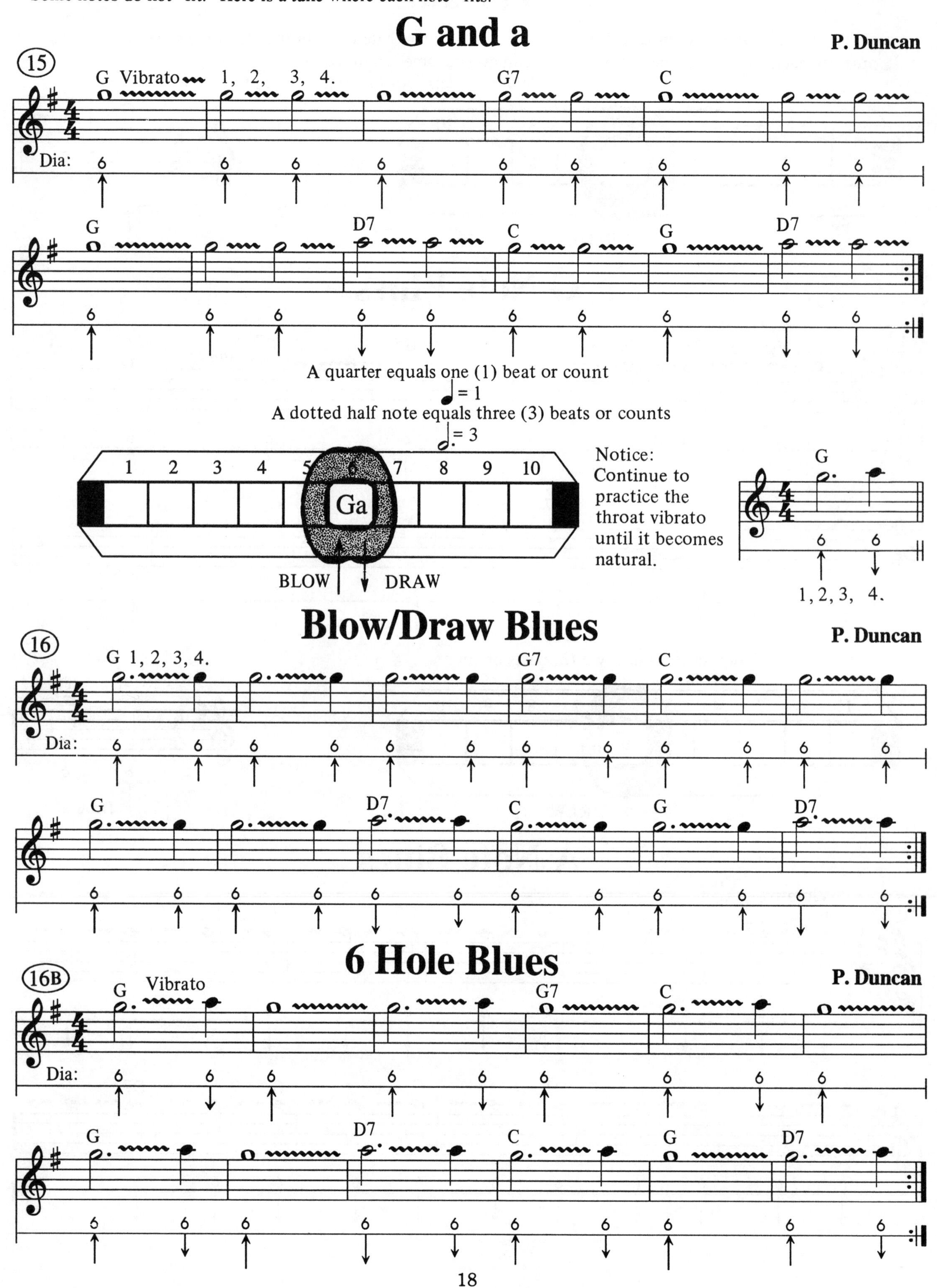

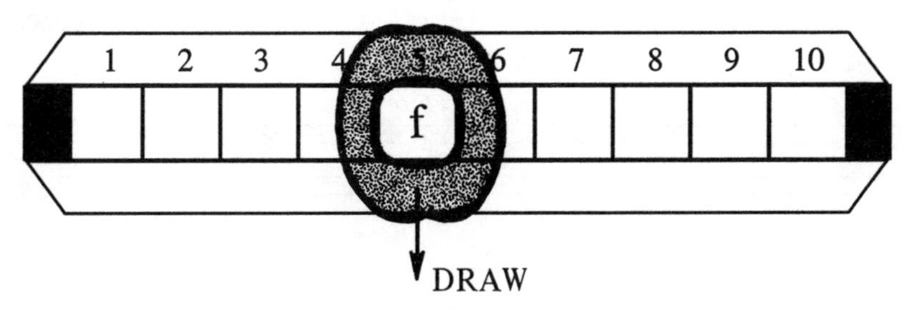

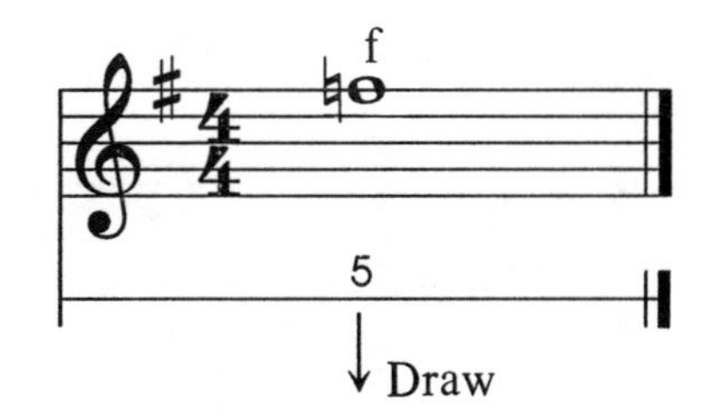

Vib Blues

P. Duncan

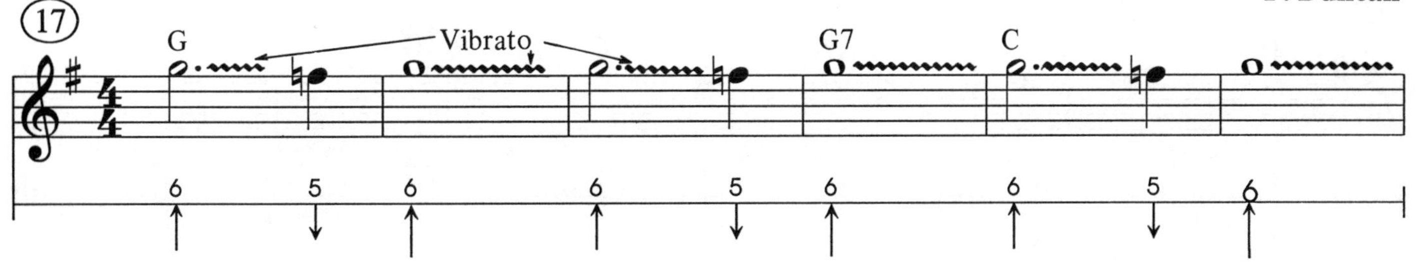

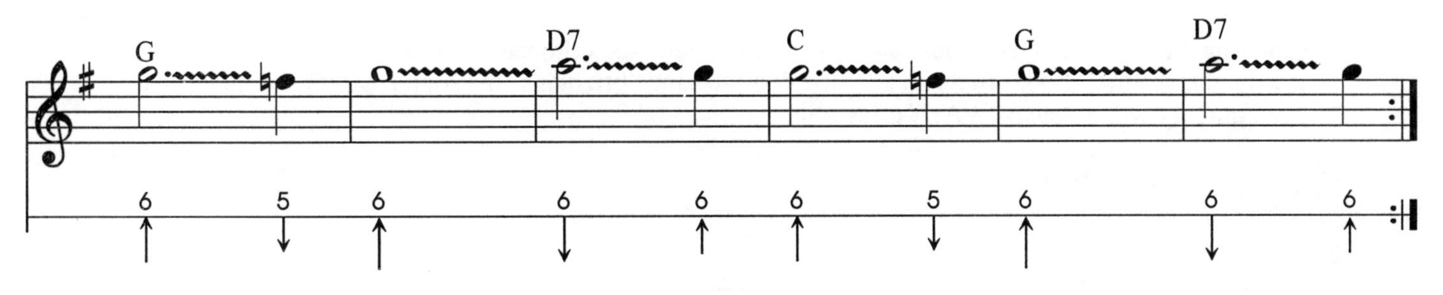

The Slide

"Glissando"

Move the harmonica from left to right, sliding or zipping the mouth across the holes from hole one to hole five. Do this while drawing air through the harmonica. Hole five is the tone you should play after the slide.

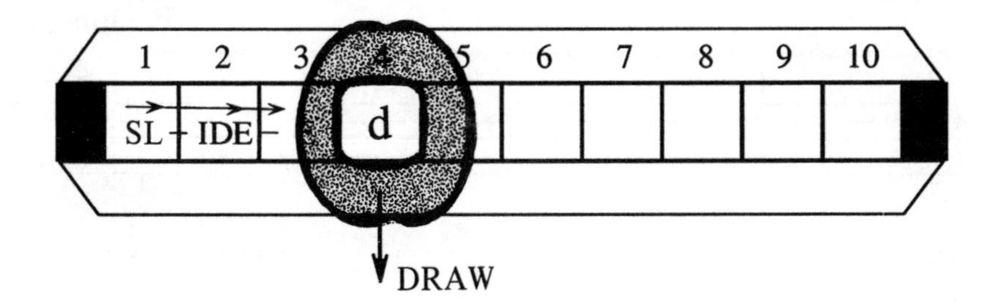

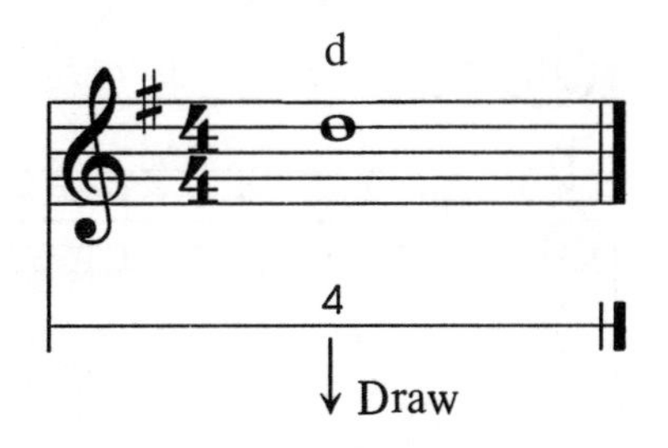

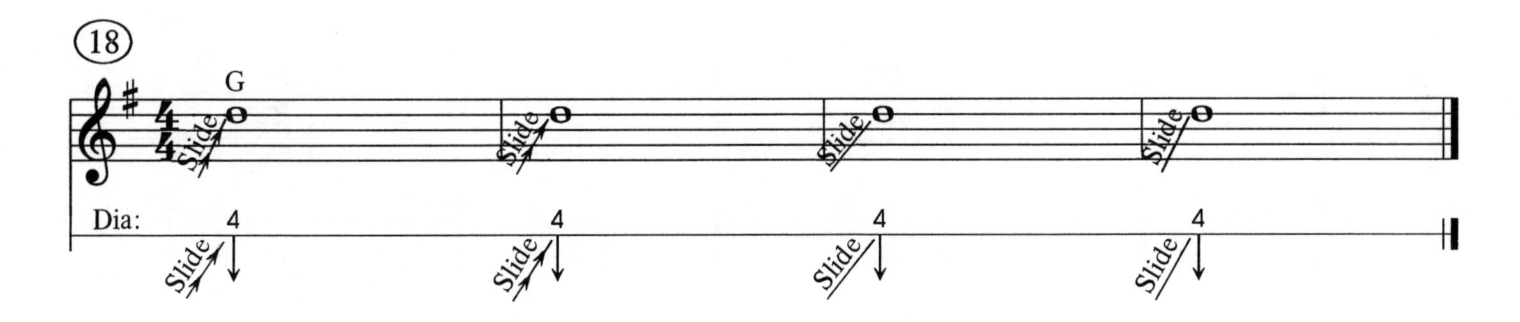

Zipp-A-Dee

P. Duncan

(19)

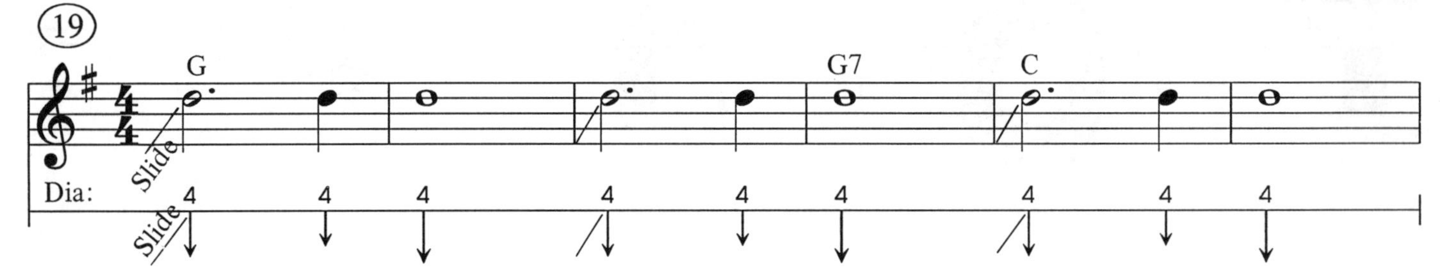

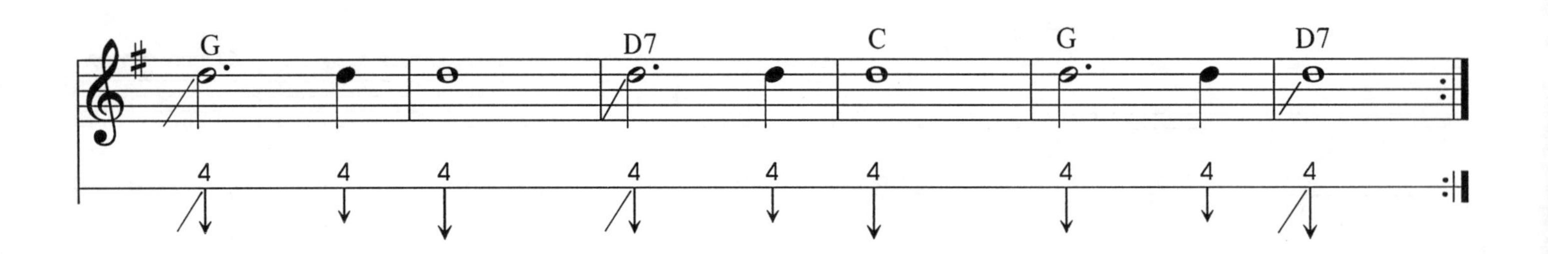

Covering the harmonica with your hand muffles the sound. Experiment with this different sound texture. It will enhance the "mood" of the tunes. Opening the hand "brightens" the sound. Moving from close to open quickly will create a "WAH" effect. See pages 6 and 7.

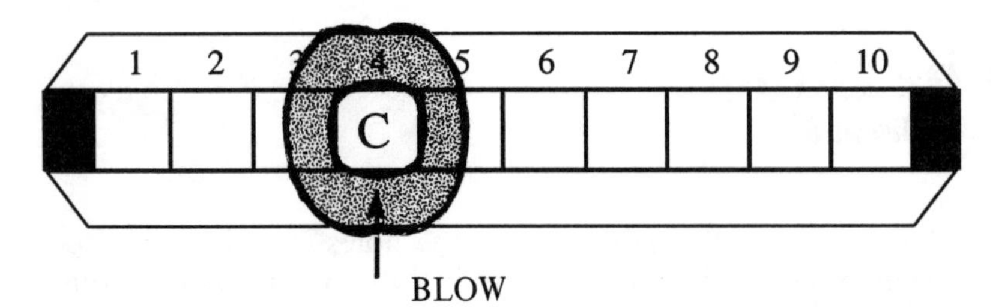

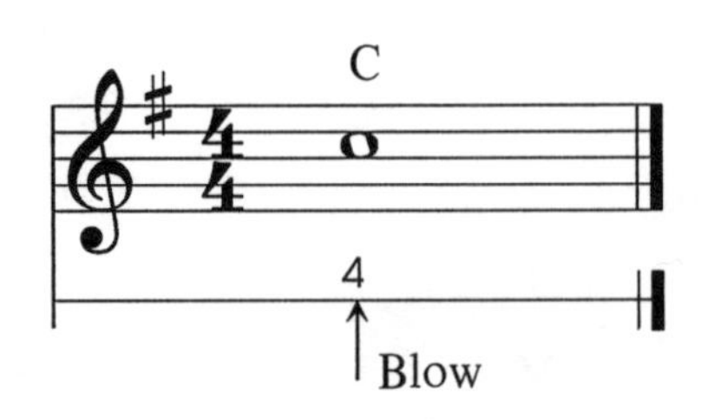

D. C. Blues

P. Duncan

(20)

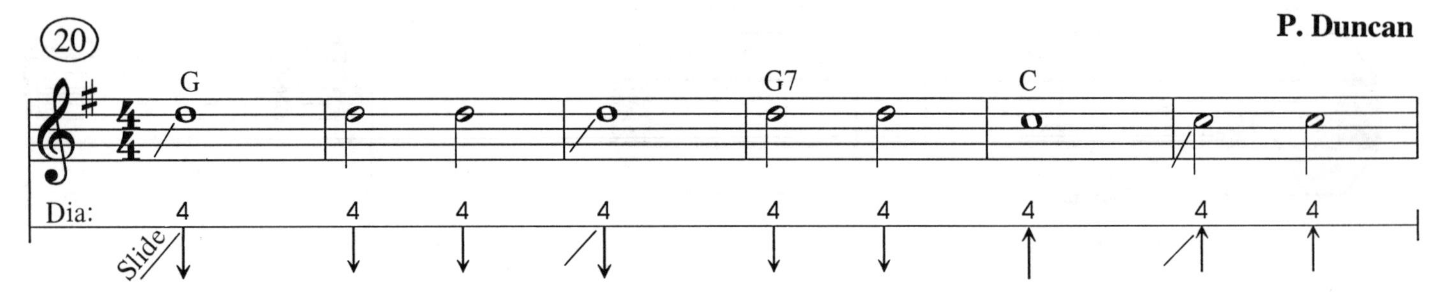

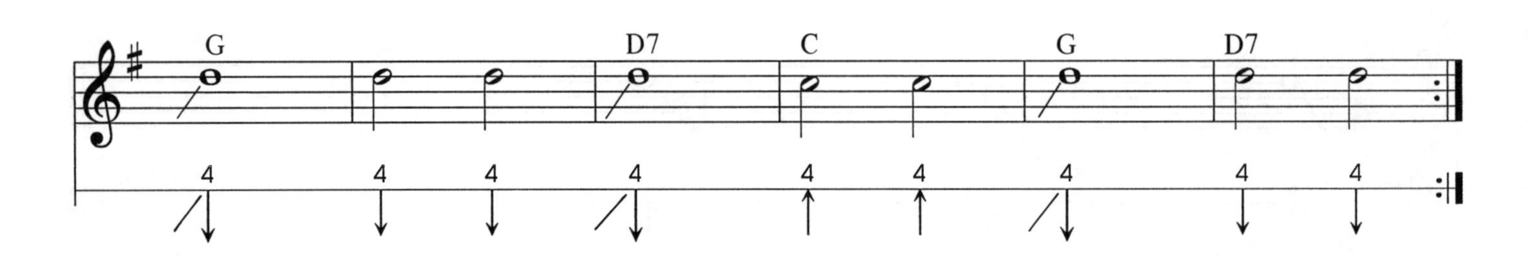

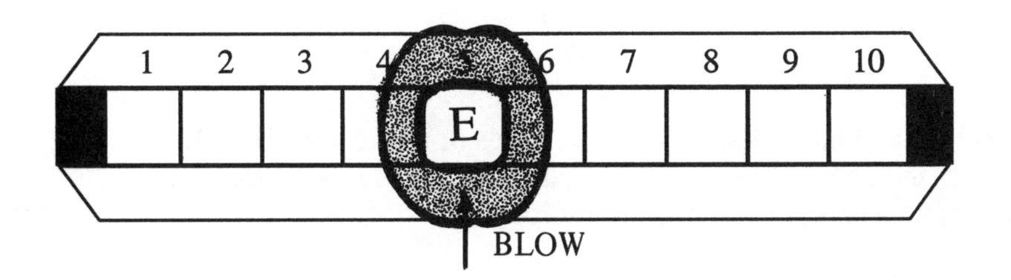

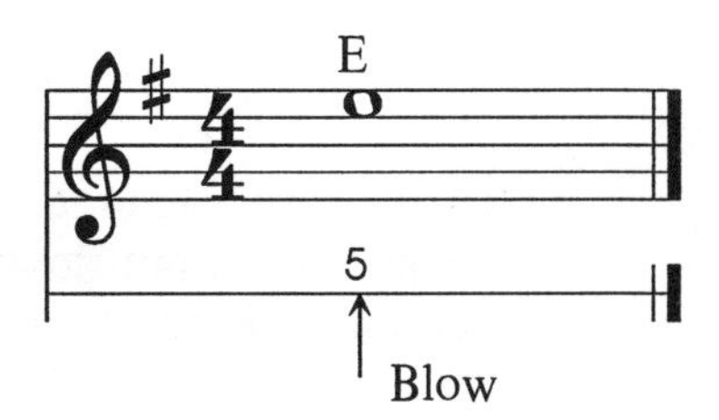

Blues "E"

P. Duncan

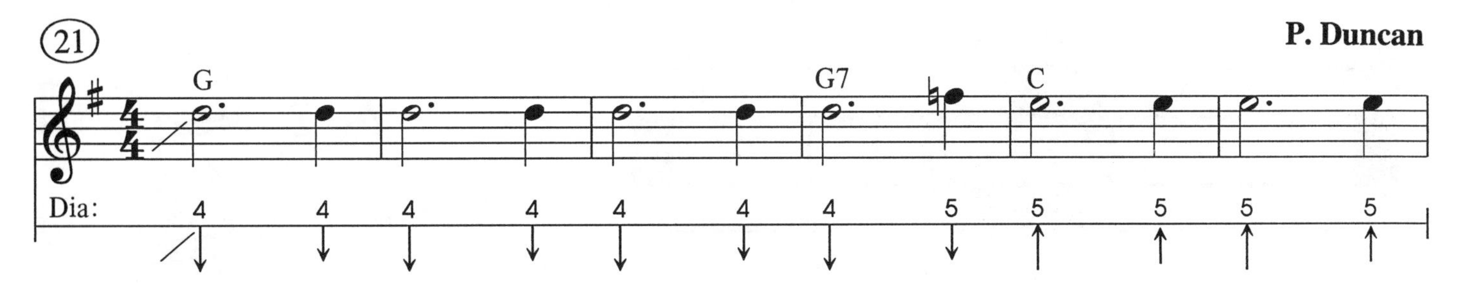

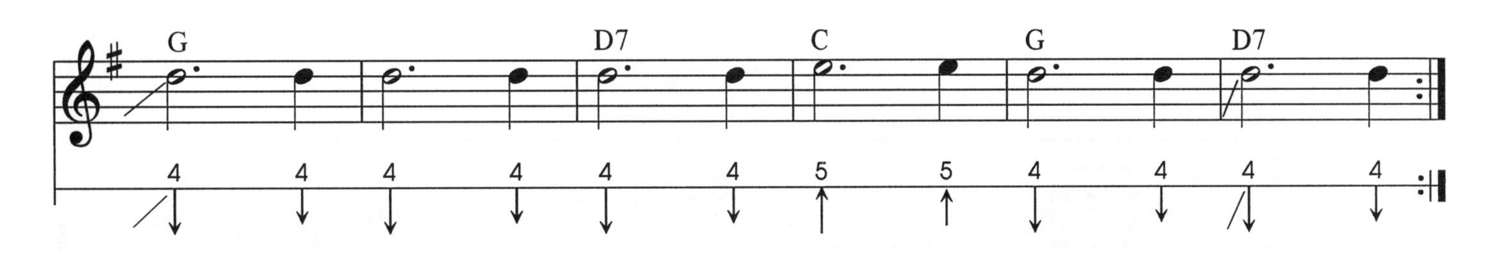

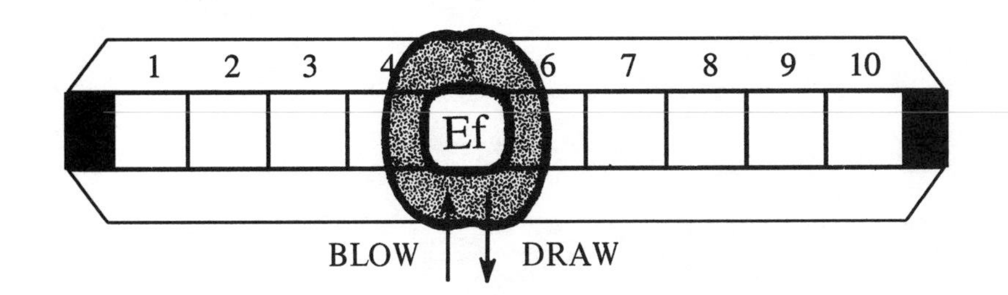

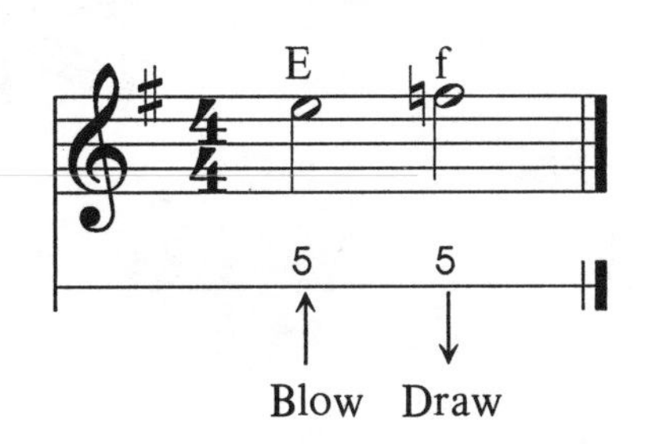

E/F Blues

P. Duncan

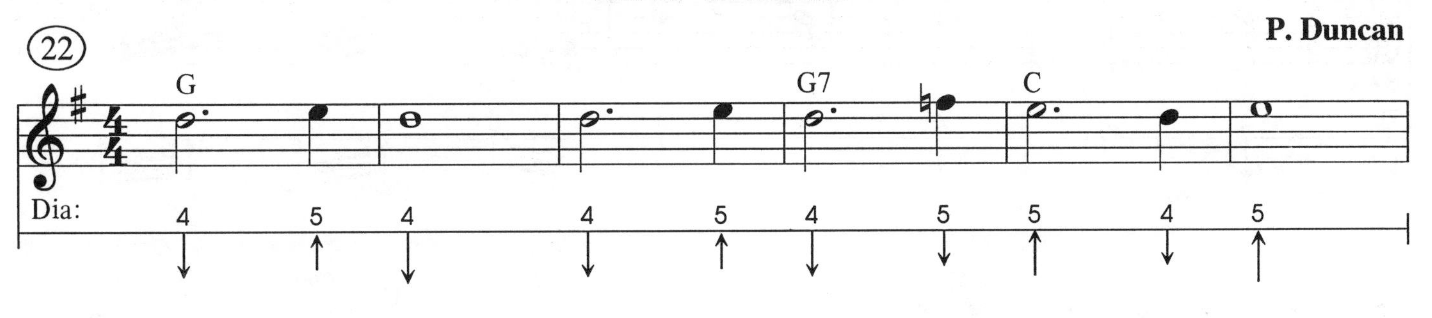

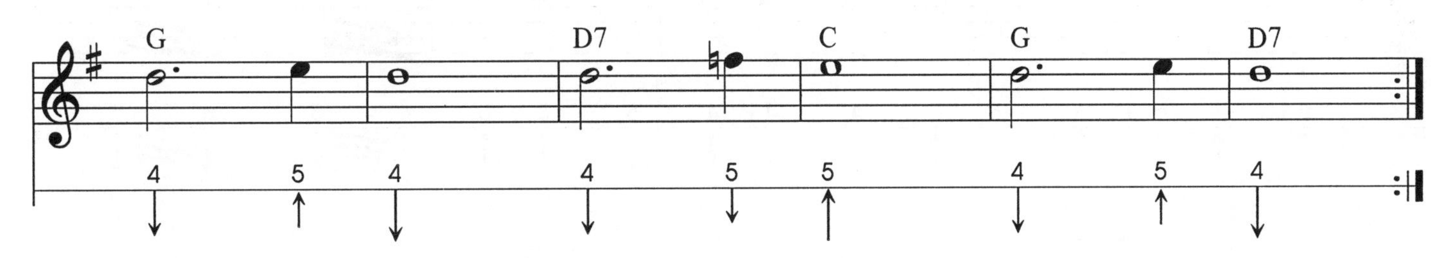

Tremolo
(Shake)

There are two ways to move from hole to hole and back again. Use your hands or shake your head like saying "No." Start slowly, steady, and even, then begin to speed up. If you lose the evenness, stop and start again. Practice and persistence will create a smooth and even tremolo.

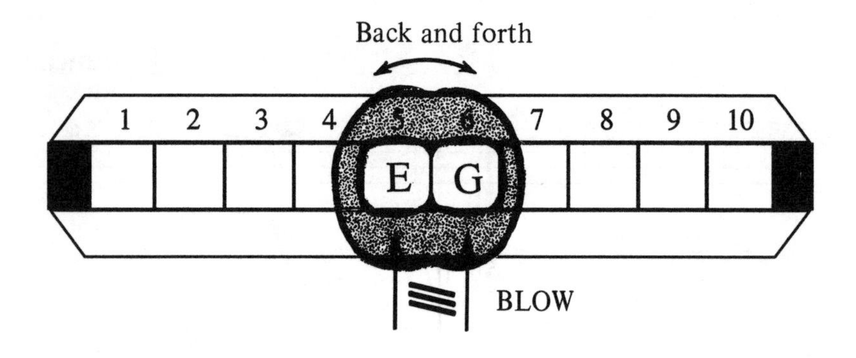

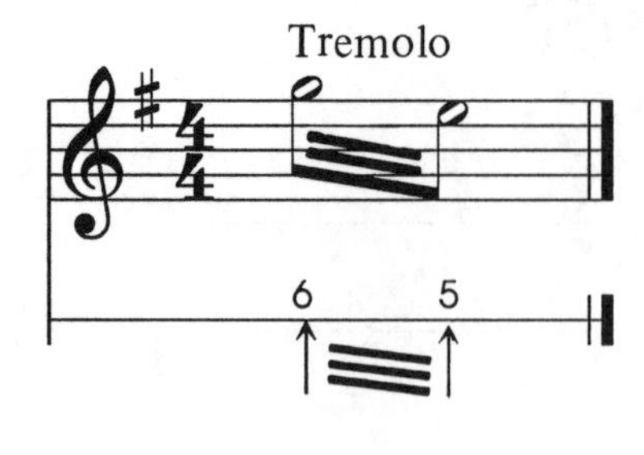

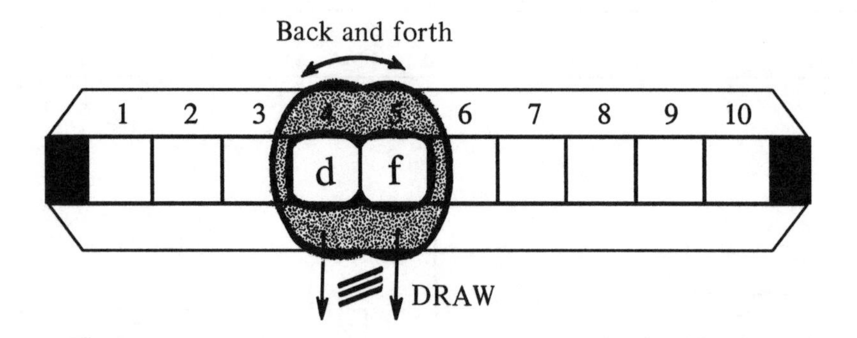

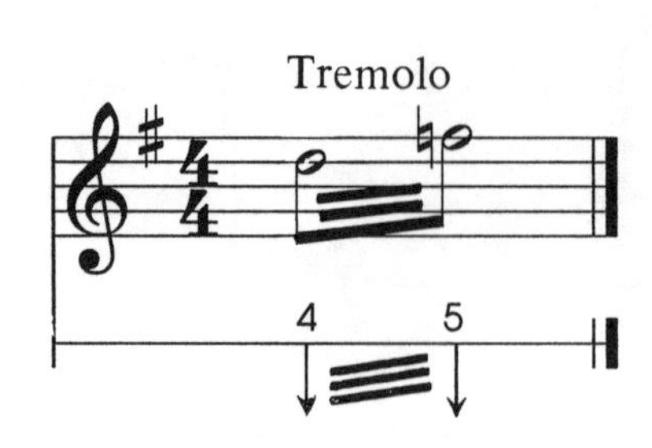

P. Duncan

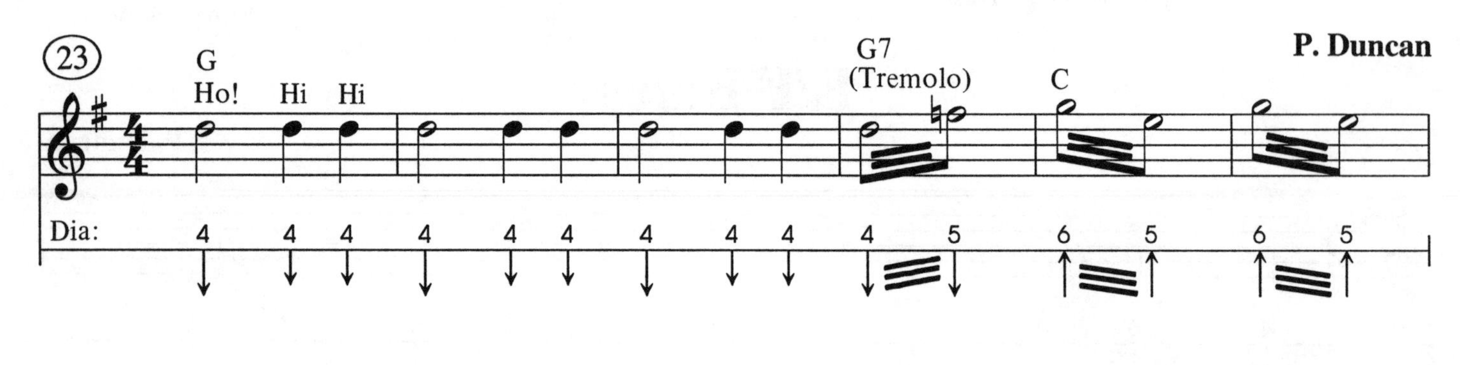

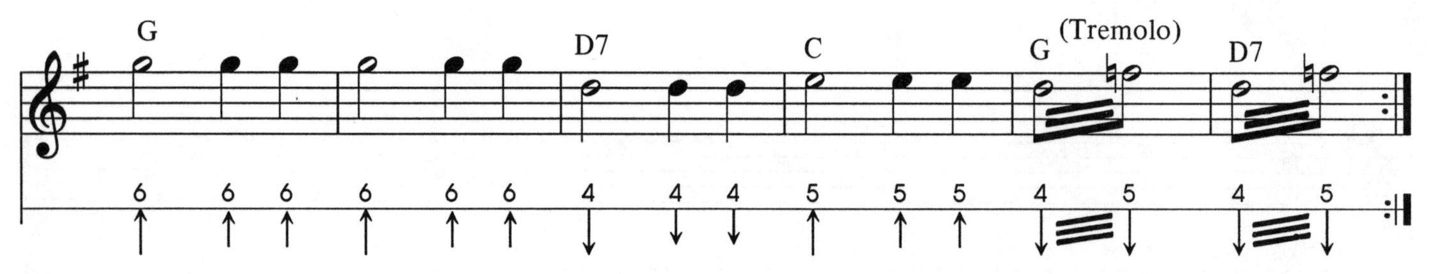

Steady Trim

Pattern Playing

= Quarter rest equals one (1) beat of silence
= Half rest equals two (2) beats of silence

Pattern One

Pattern Two

Pattern Three

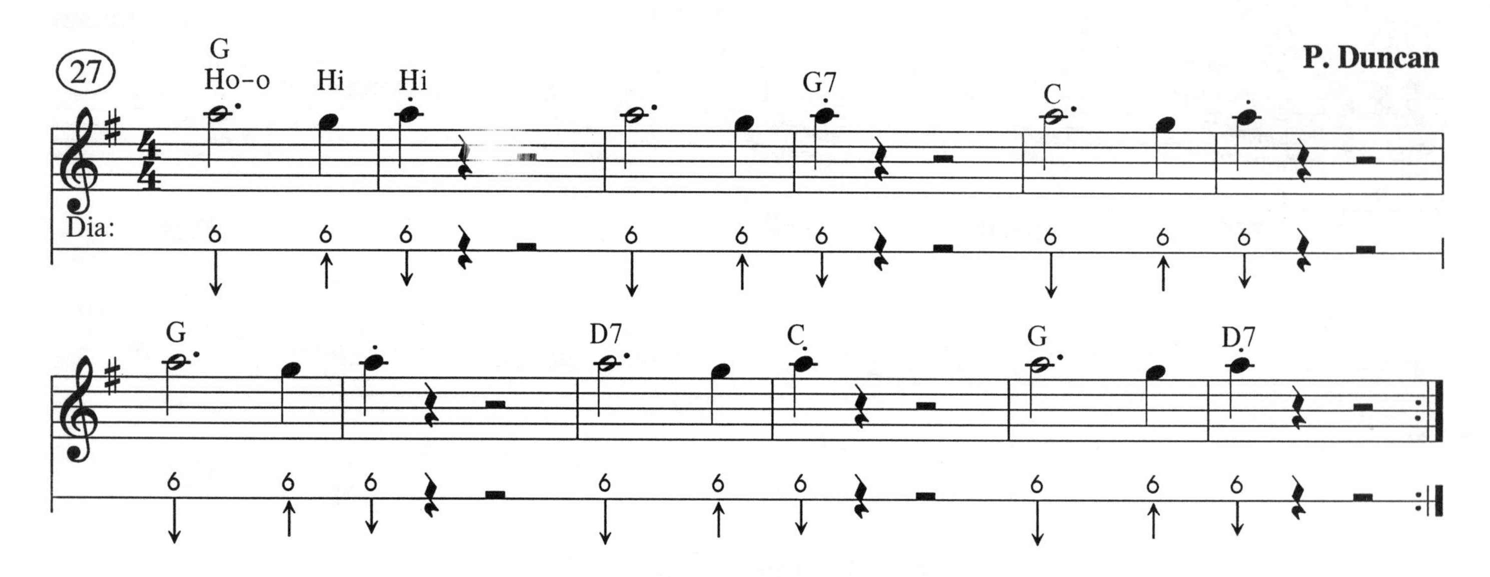

These patterns are interchangeable — they may be played anywhere in the 12-bar blues form. Here is an example.

Combination

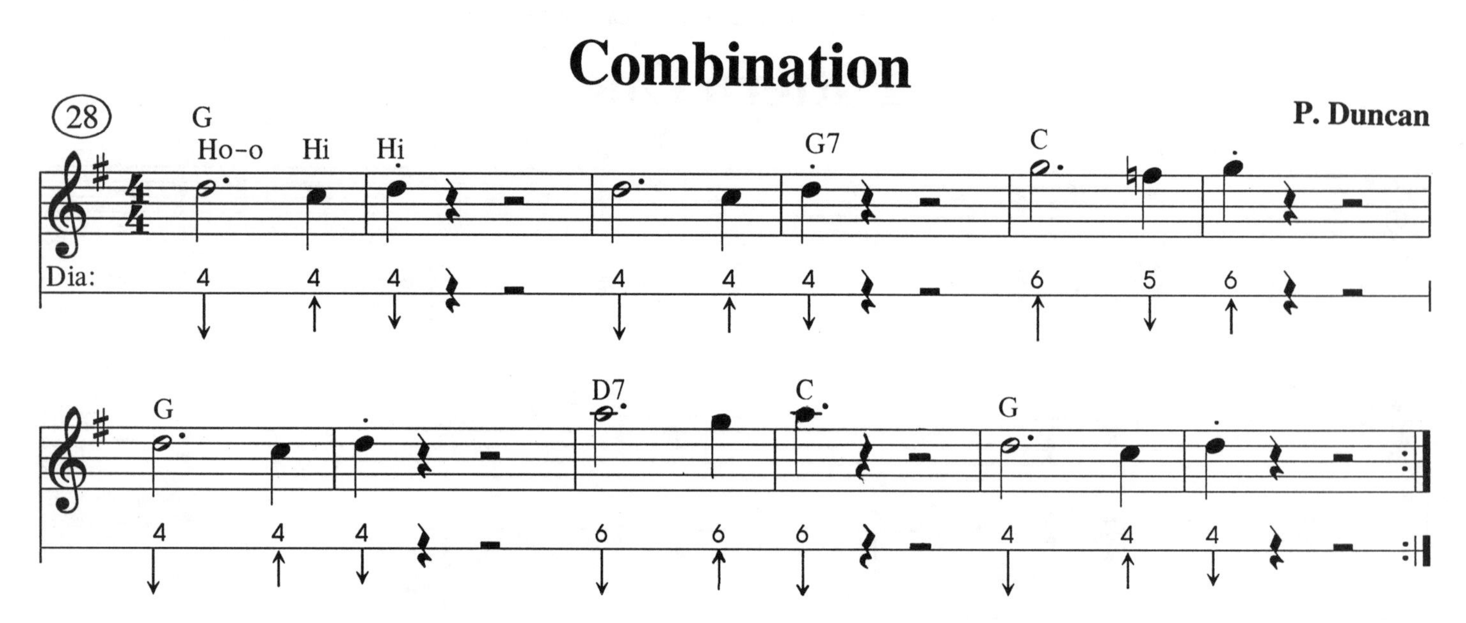

Variation I

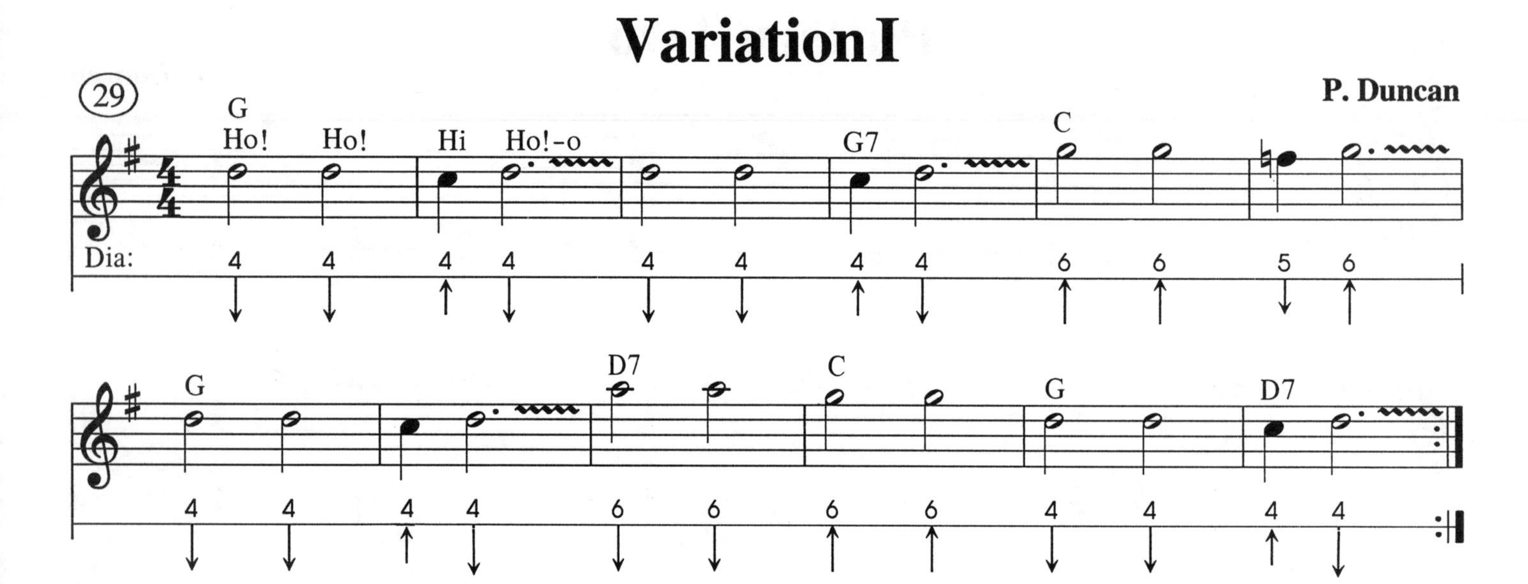

Variation II

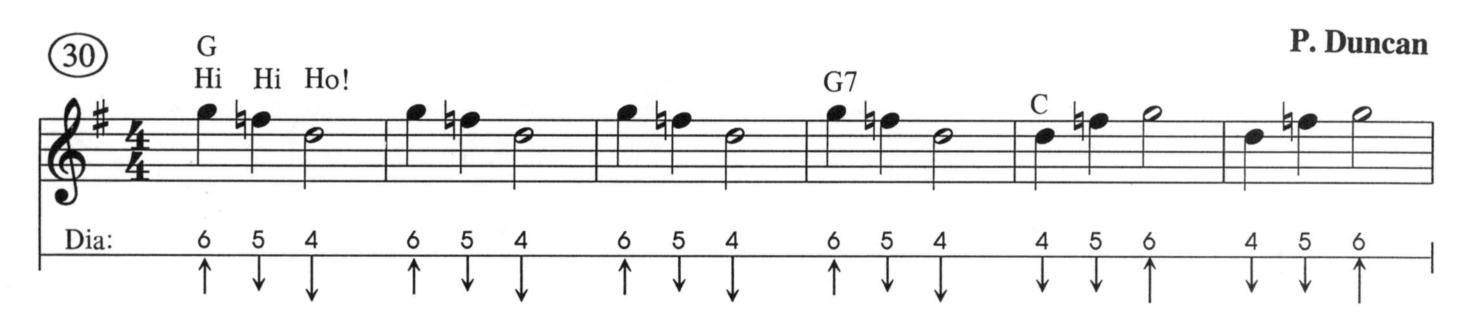

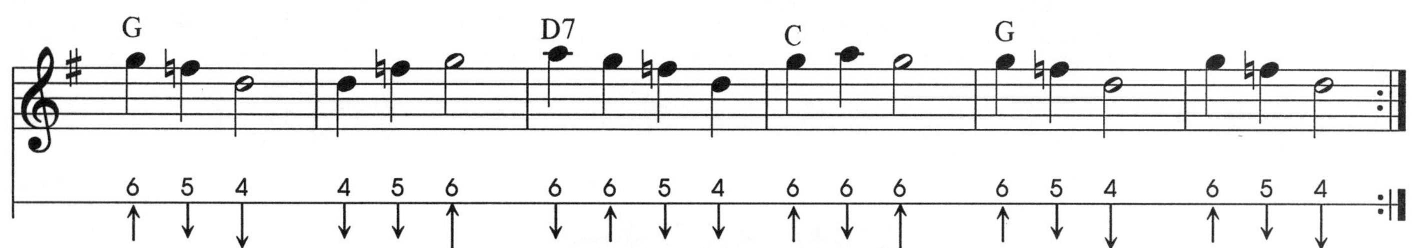

Faster Patterns

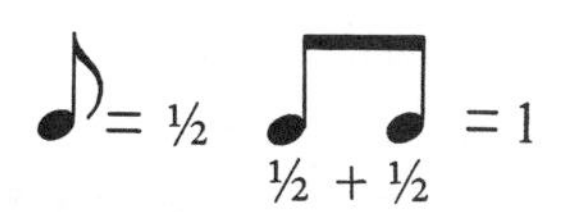

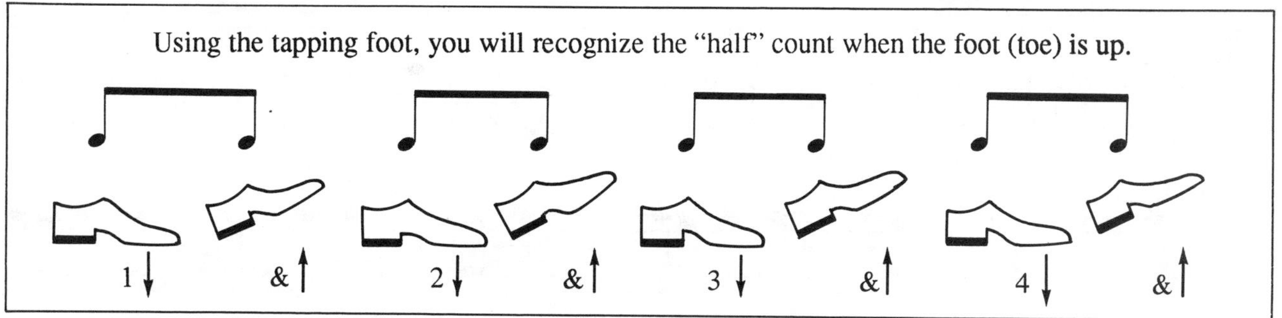

Tapping your foot will help keep the rhythm steady.

Pattern One

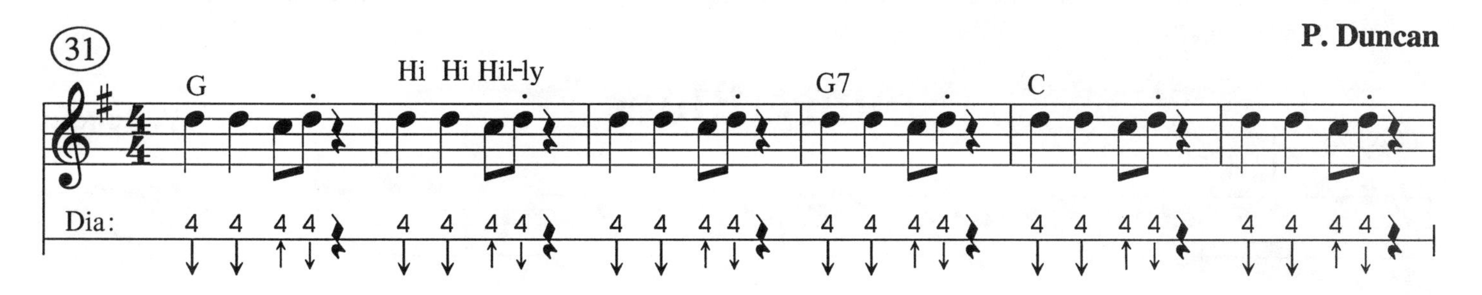

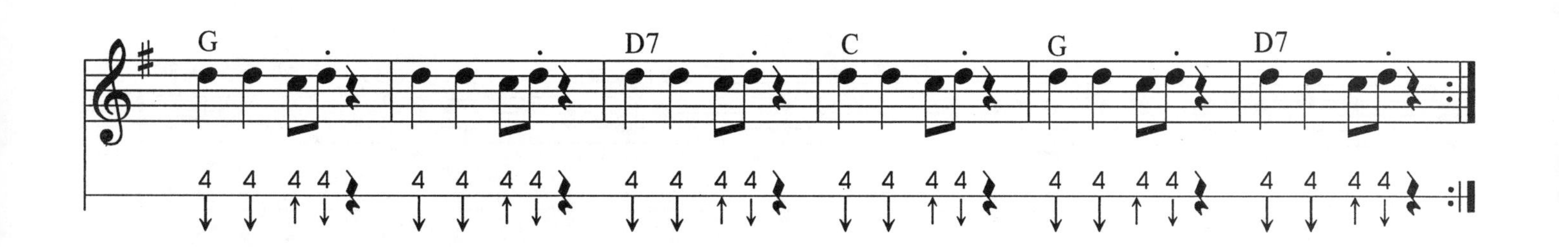

Pattern Two

P. Duncan

32

Pattern Three

P. Duncan

33

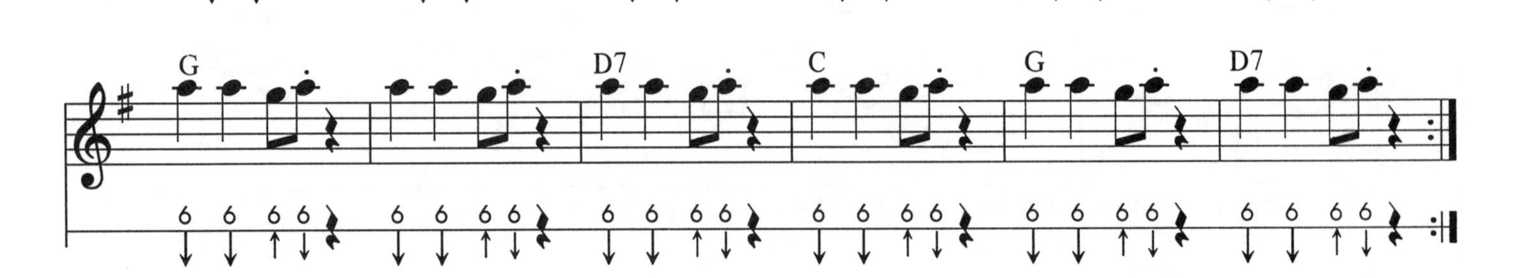

These patterns are interchangeable — they may be played anywhere within the 12-bar blues form. Here is an example.

Bounce Blues

P. Duncan

34

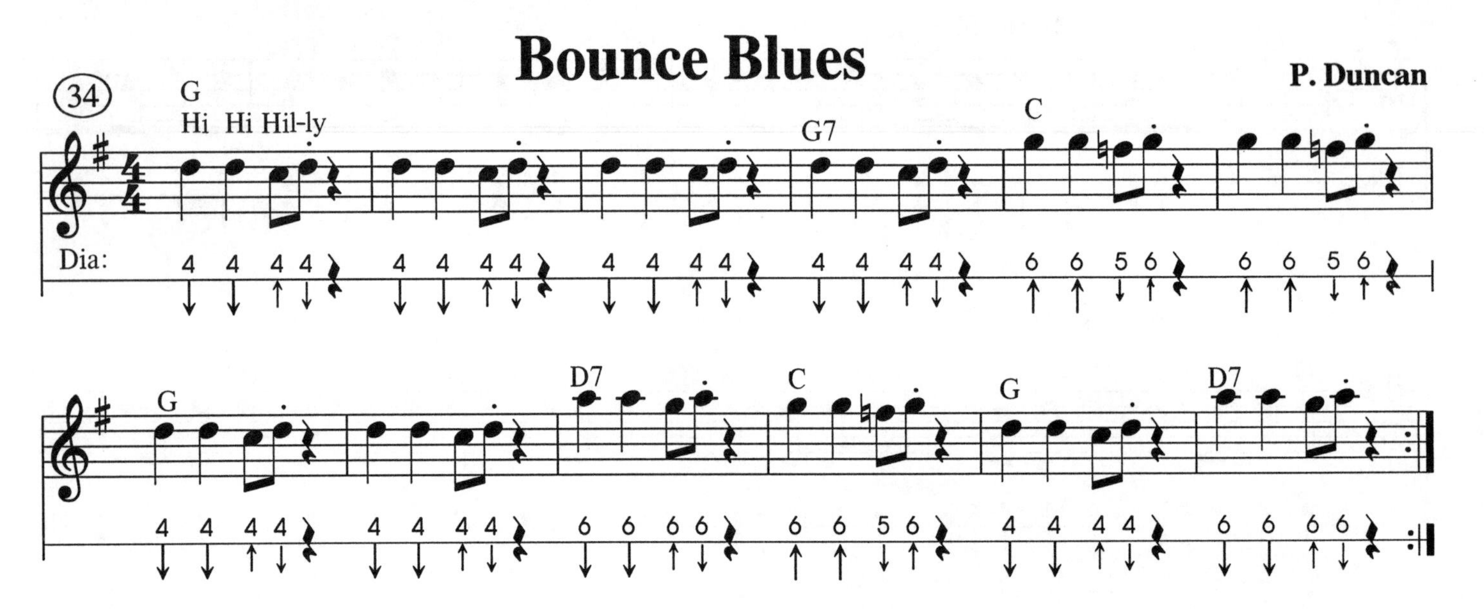

More Patterns

These interchangeable patterns can be played even or in a shuffle style. Practice each pattern 50 times each day.

Pattern One

P. Duncan

35

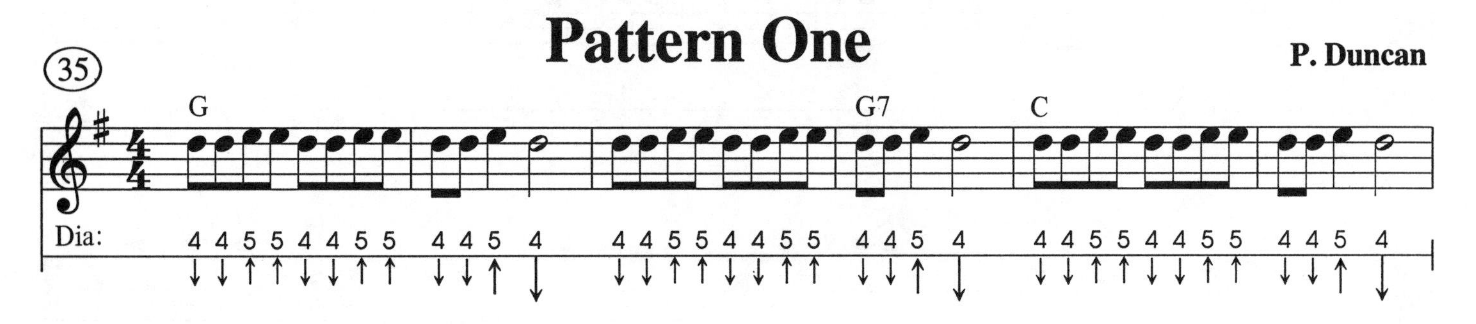

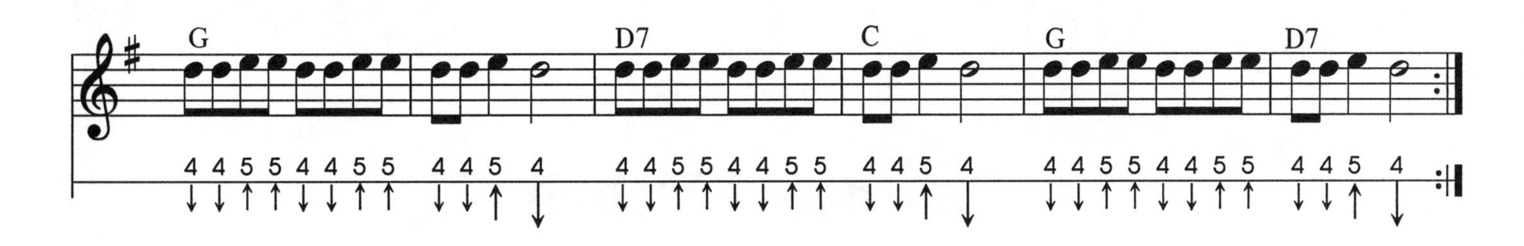

Pattern Two

P. Duncan

36

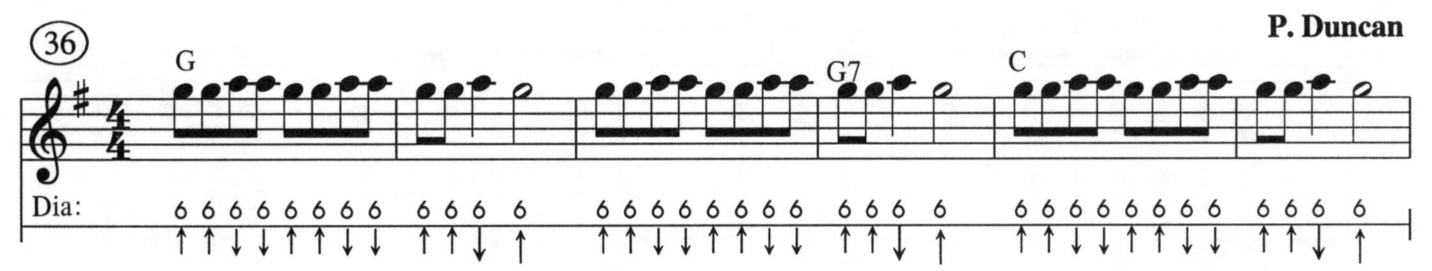

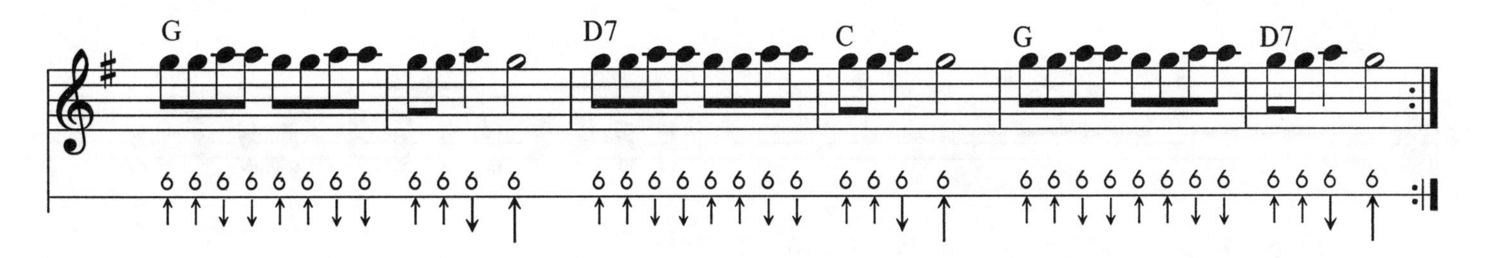

Cut time: Two (2) beats per measure

More Patterns

37

38

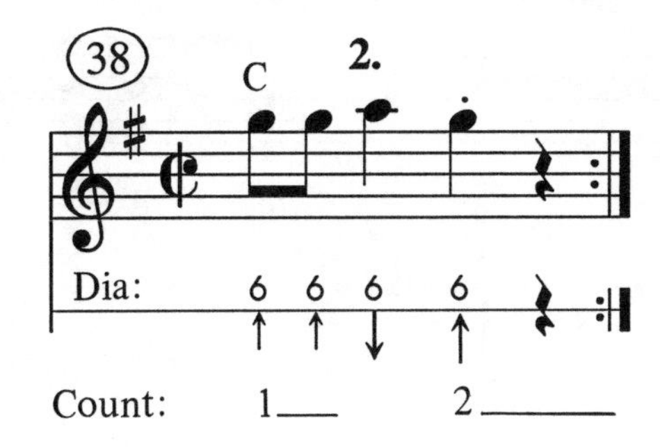

39

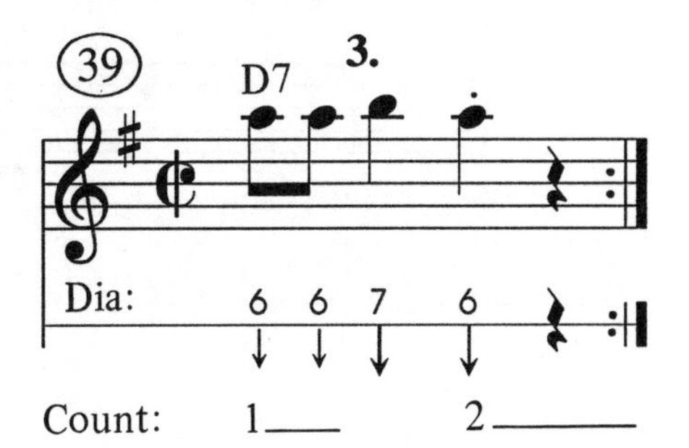

Combination

P. Duncan

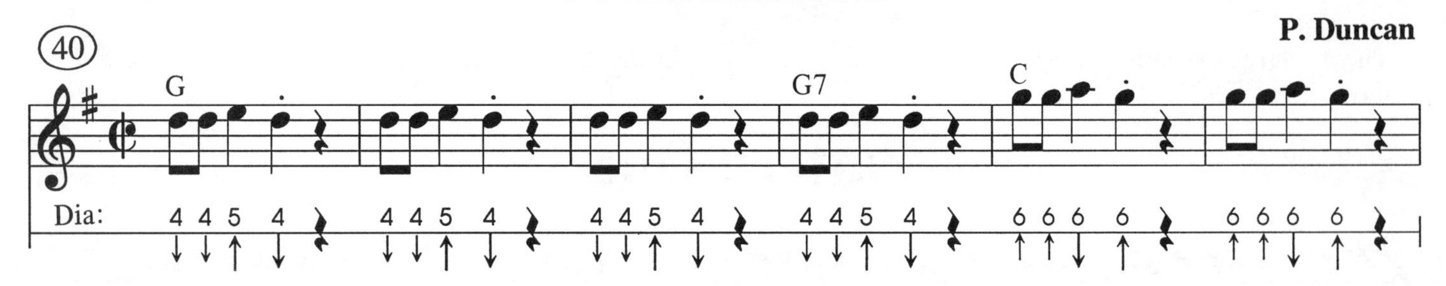

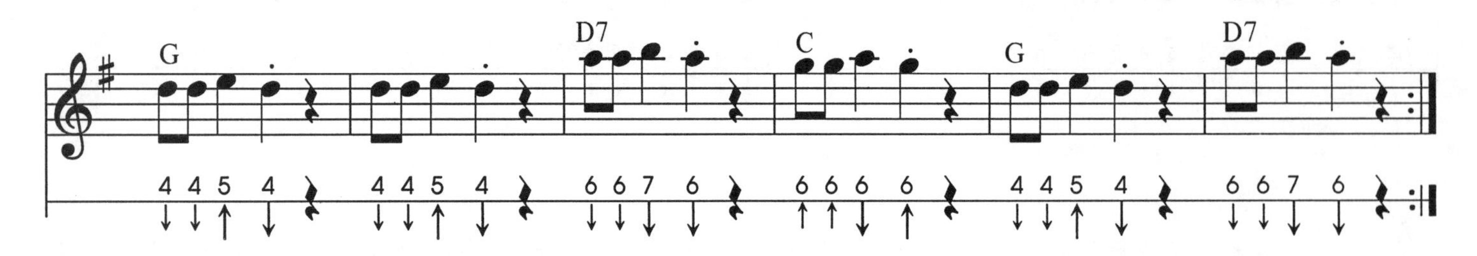

Chord and Melody

Played:

¢ = Cut time
2/2 time

Driven Rhythm

P. Duncan

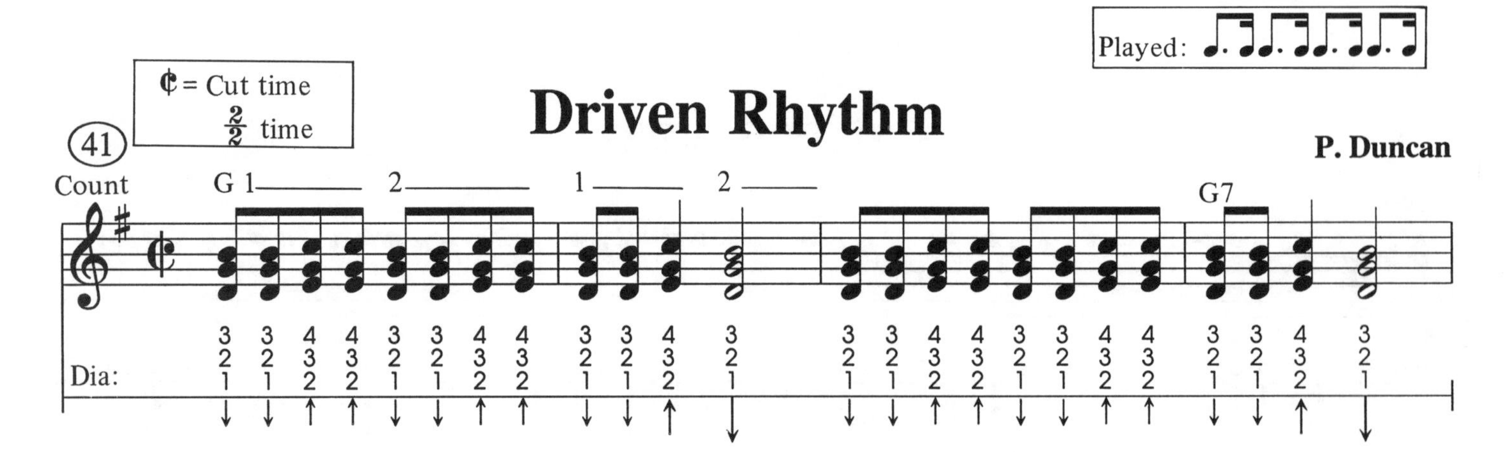

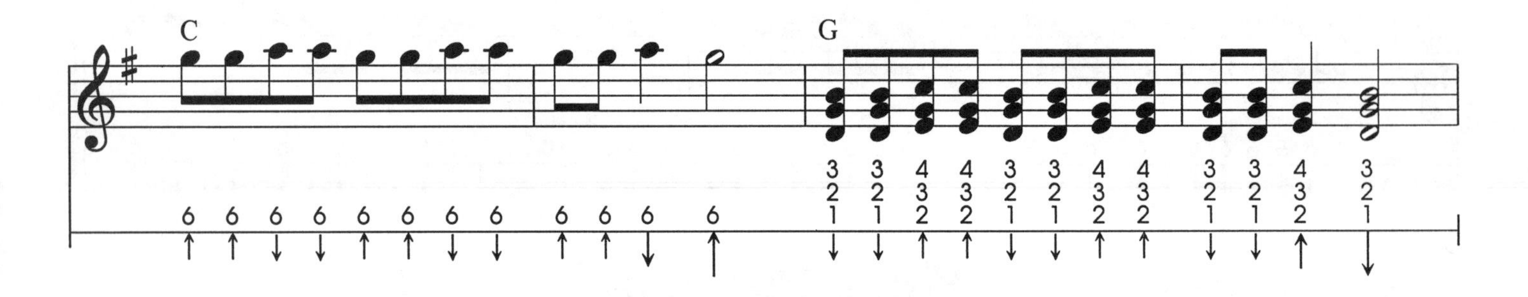

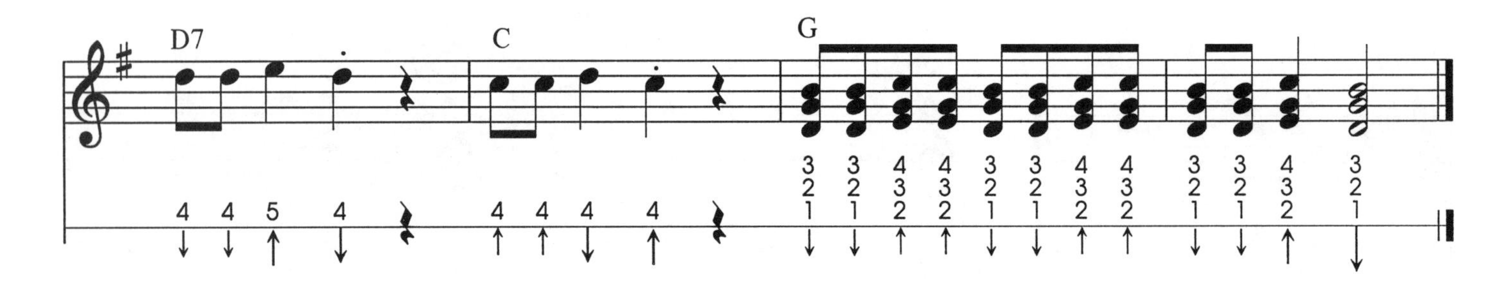

Harmonica Shuffle

(Play this with a Friend)

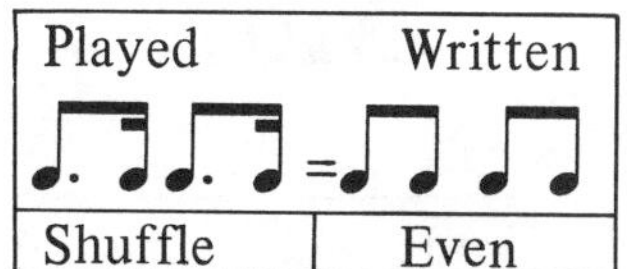

P. Duncan

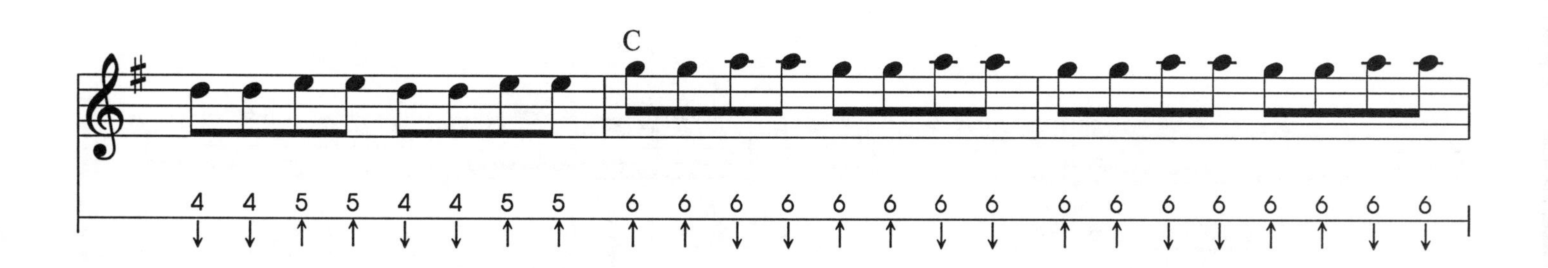

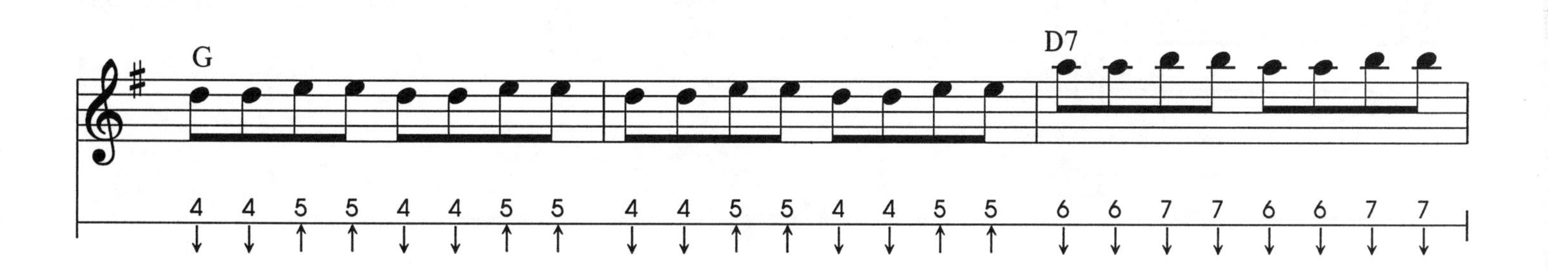

More Patterns That Can Remain The Same

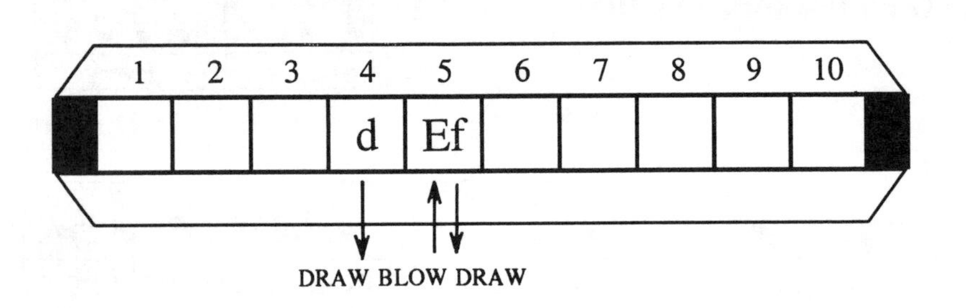

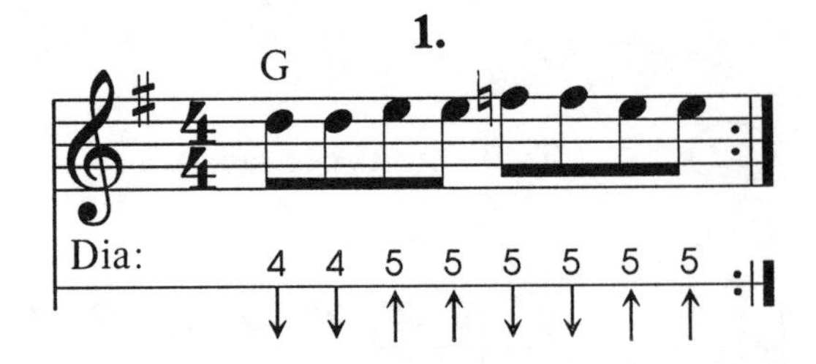

One

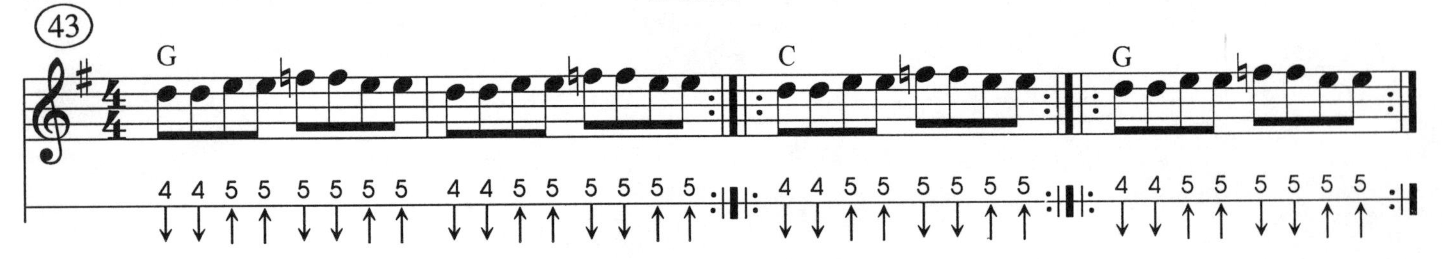

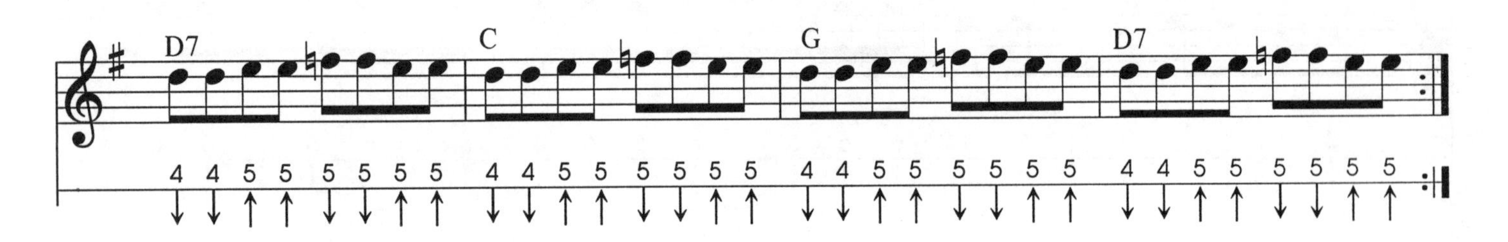

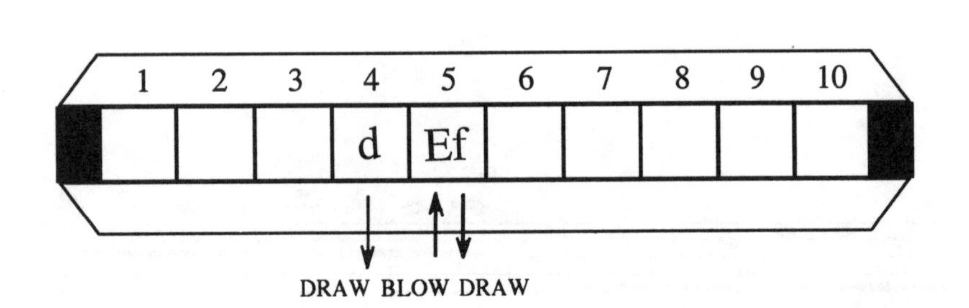

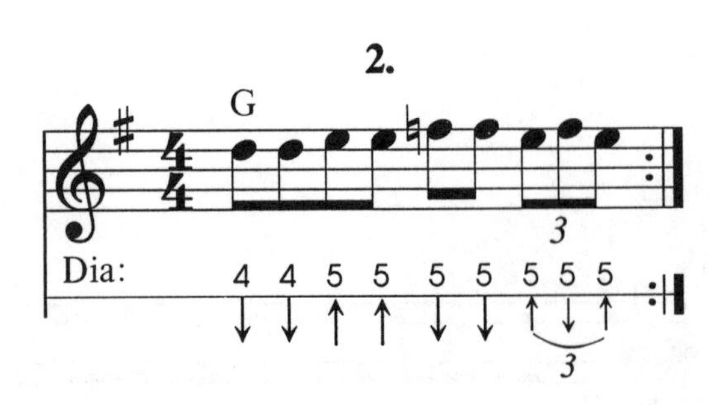

Two

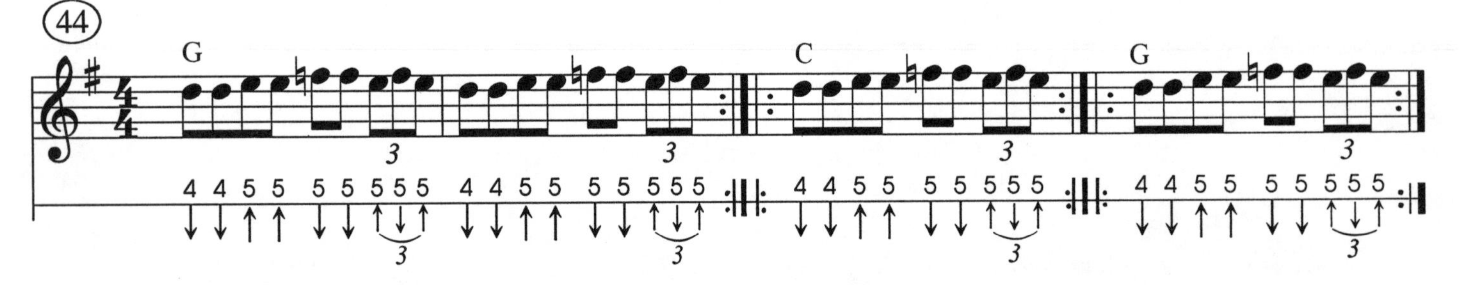

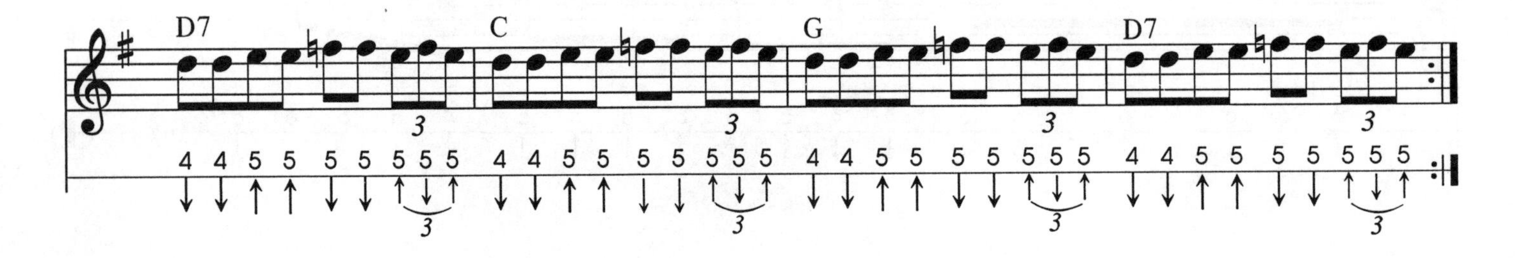

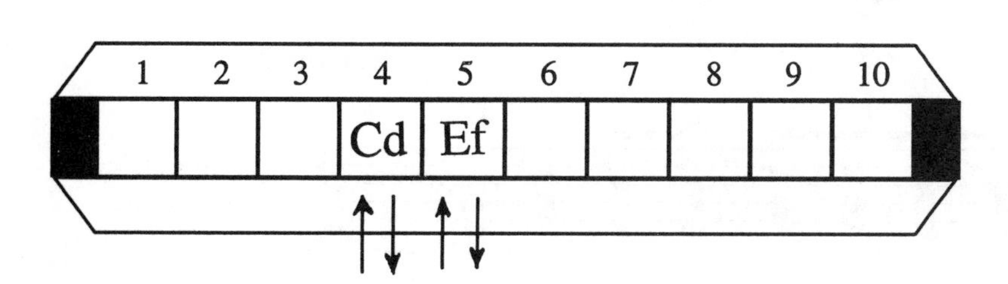
1 2 3 4 5 6 7 8 9 10
Cd Ef

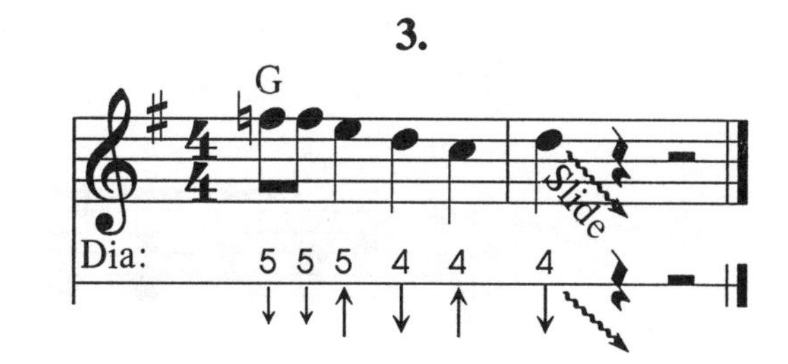
3.
G
Slide
Dia:
5 5 5 4 4 4

Three

45
G G7 C
Dia:
5 5 5 4 4 4 5 5 5 4 4 4 5 5 5 4 4 4

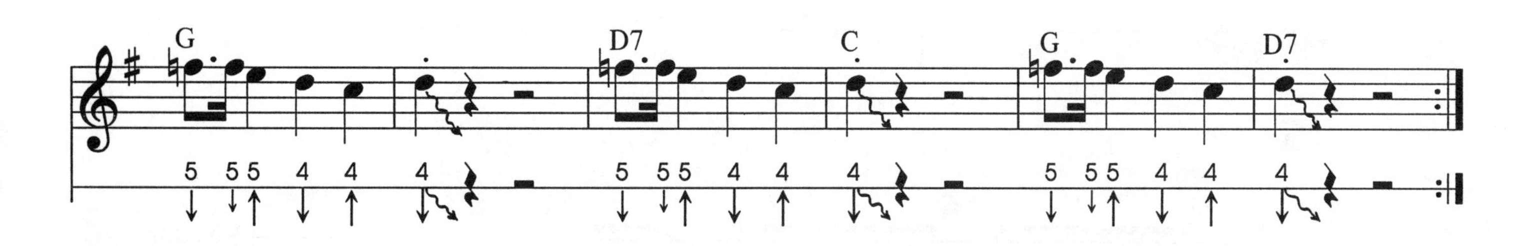
G D7 C G D7
5 5 5 4 4 4 5 5 5 4 4 4 5 5 5 4 4 4

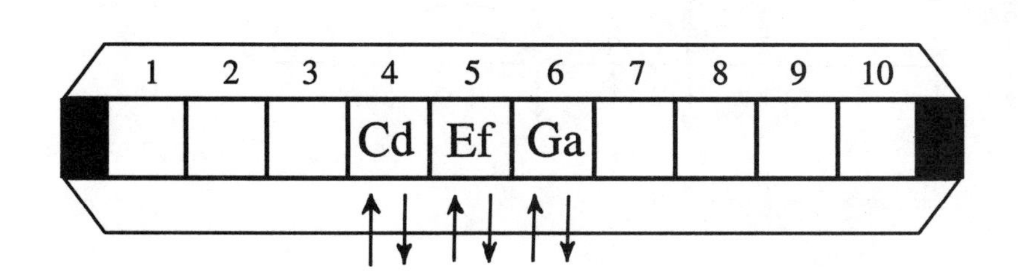
1 2 3 4 5 6 7 8 9 10
Cd Ef Ga

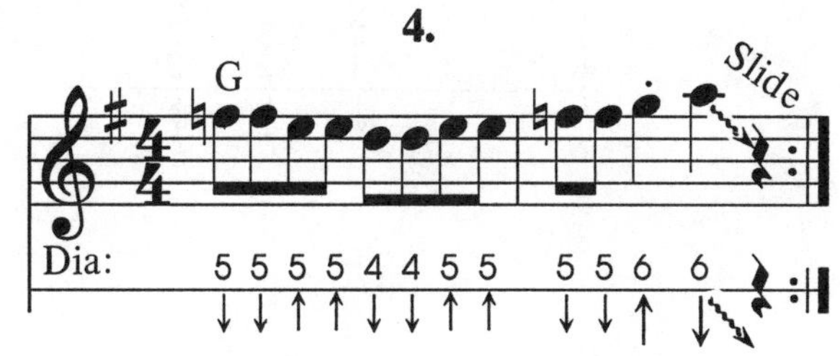
4.
G
Slide
Dia:
5 5 5 5 4 4 5 5 5 5 6 6

Four

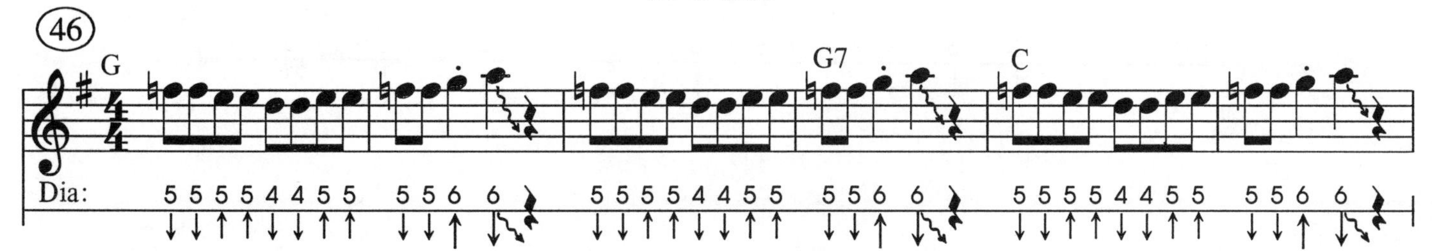
46
G G7 C
Dia:
5 5 5 5 4 4 5 5 5 5 6 6 5 5 5 5 4 4 5 5 5 5 6 6 5 5 5 5 4 4 5 5 5 5 6 6

G D7 C G D7
5 5 5 5 4 4 5 5 5 5 6 6 5 5 5 5 4 4 5 5 5 5 6 6 5 5 5 5 4 4 5 5 5 5 6 6

Swing Blues

(47)

P. Duncan

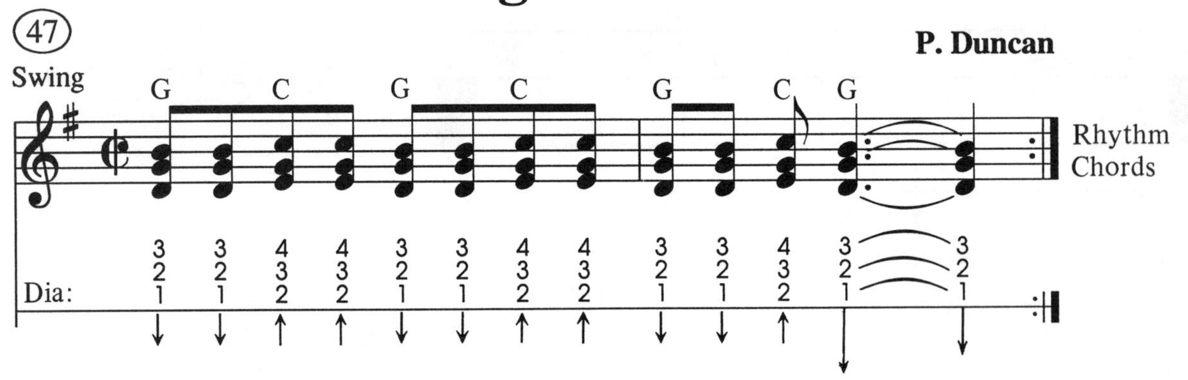

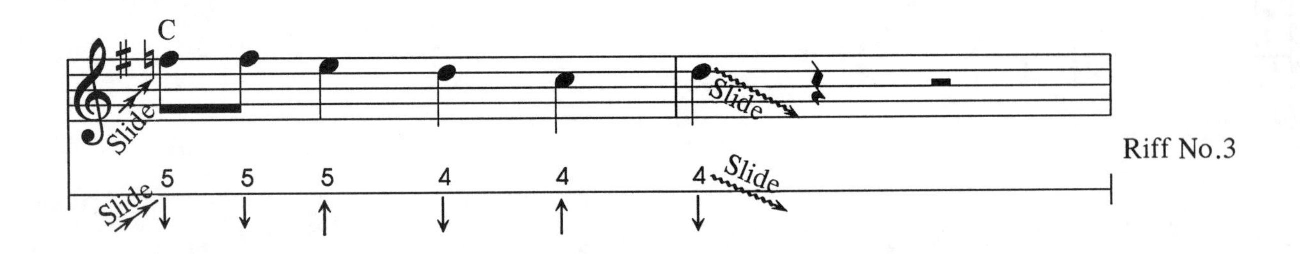

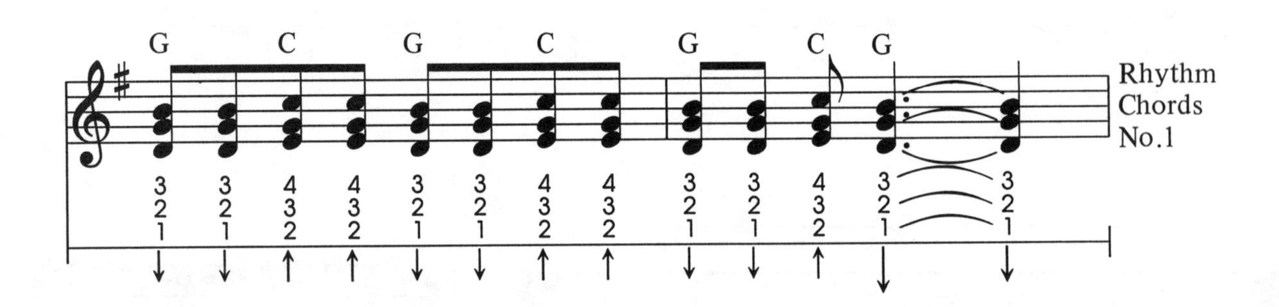

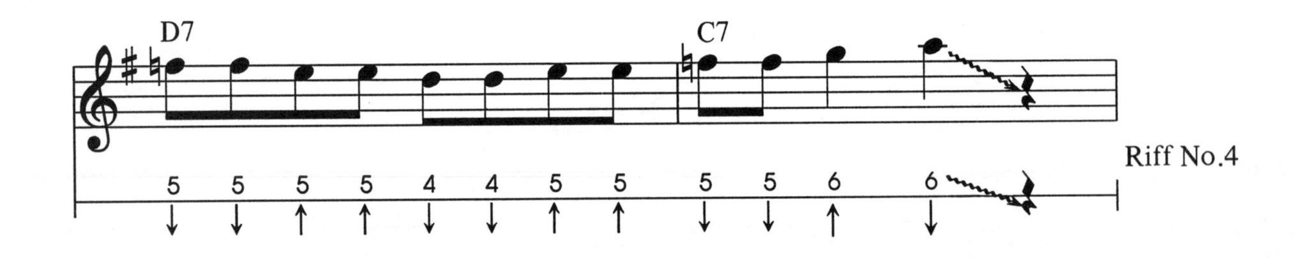

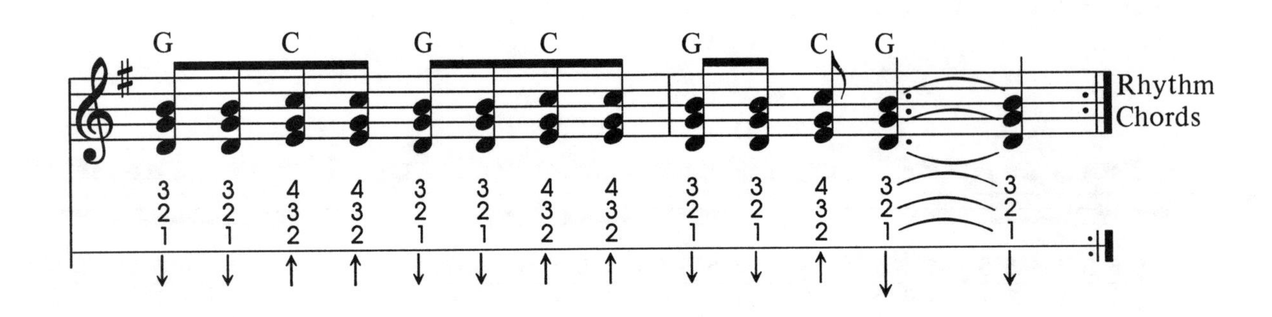

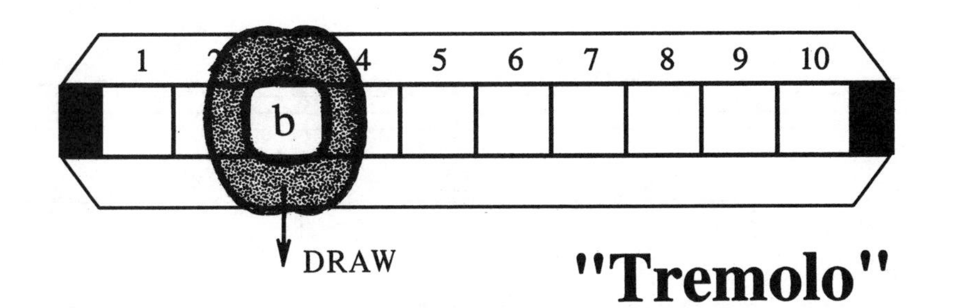

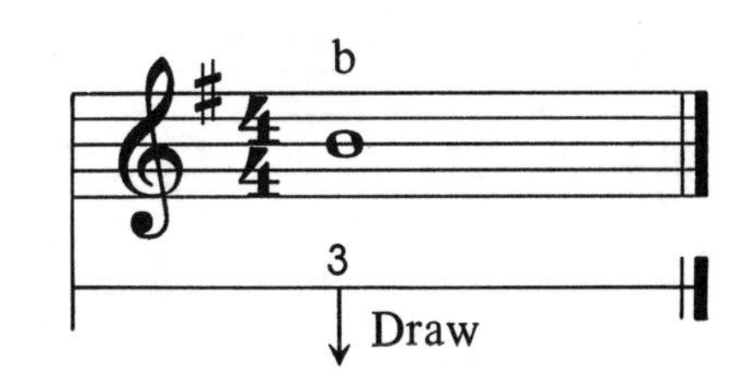

"Tremolo"

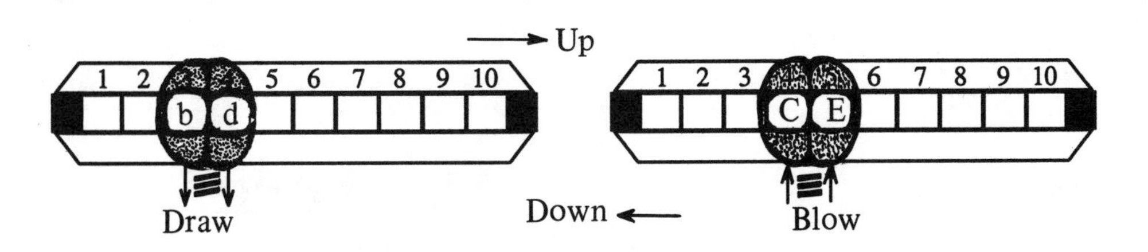

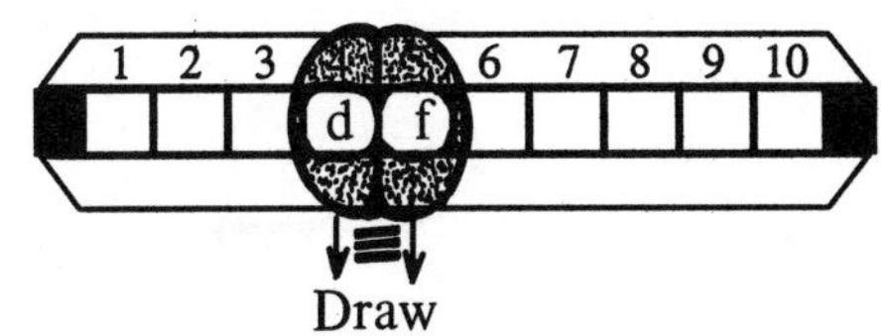

Movin' Tremolo

P. Duncan

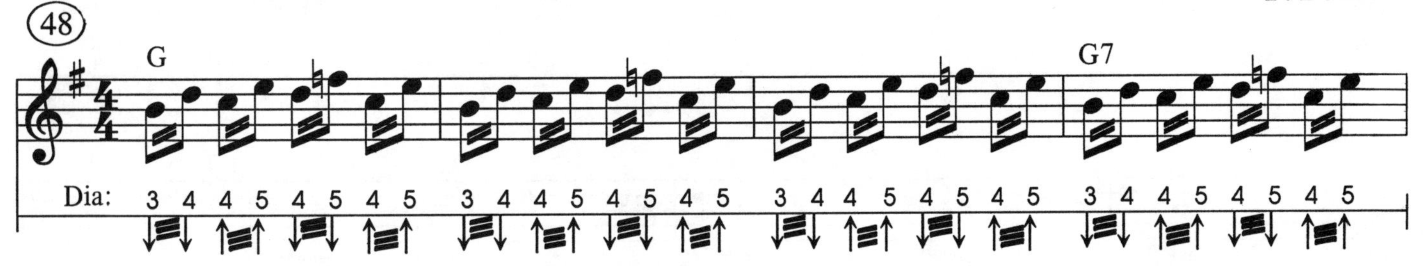

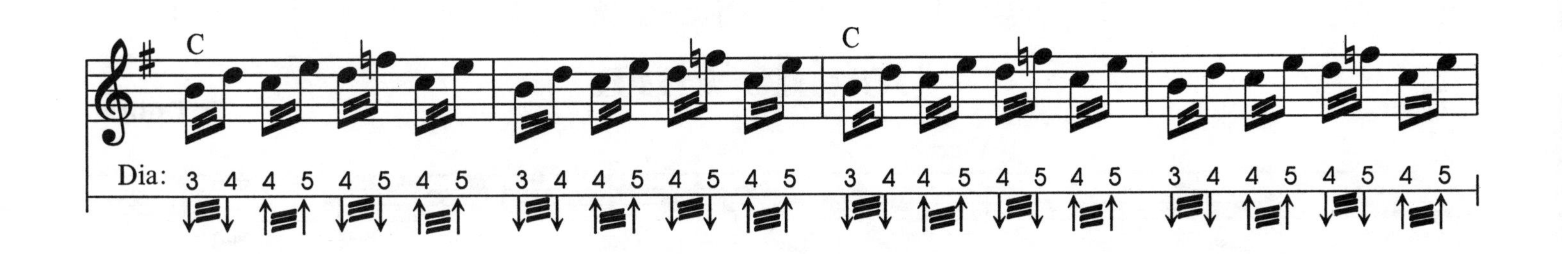

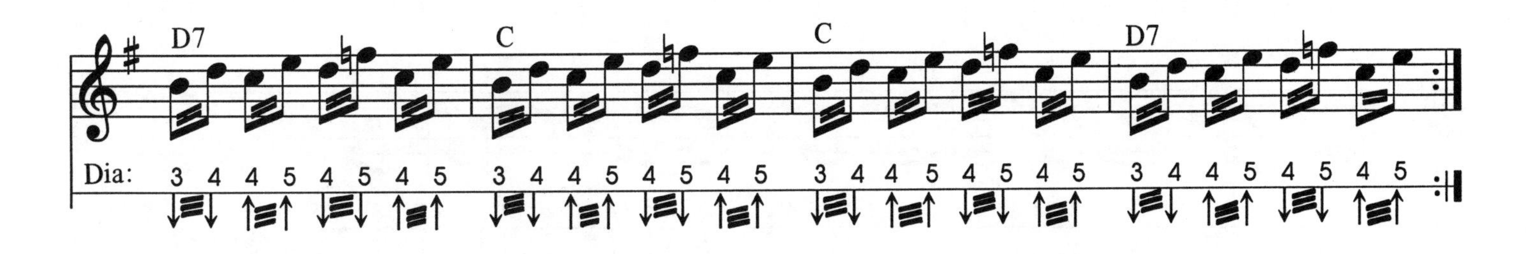

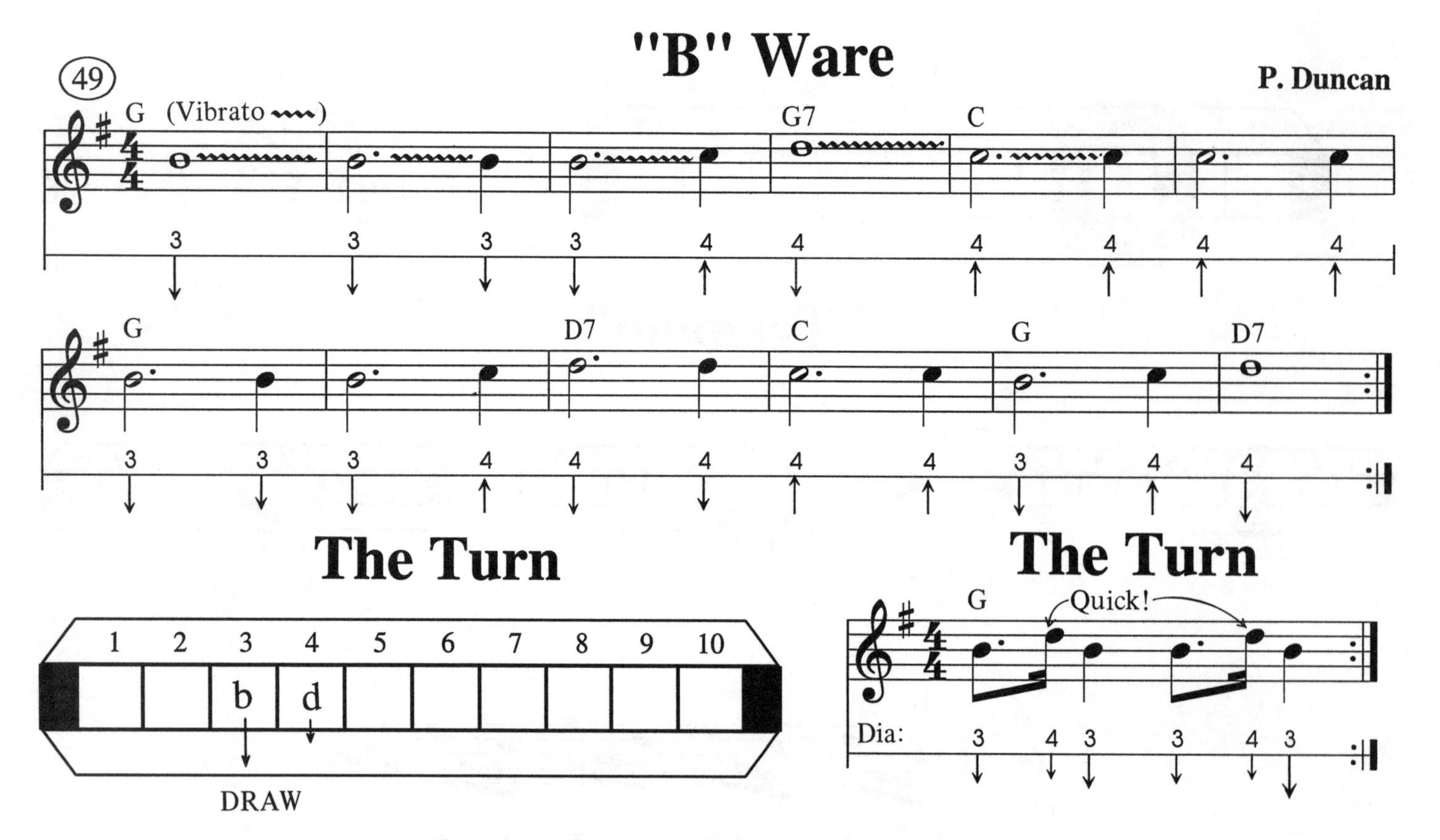

The middle tone is real quick. You just rock the harp and quickly touch the upper tone, then back to the first tone.

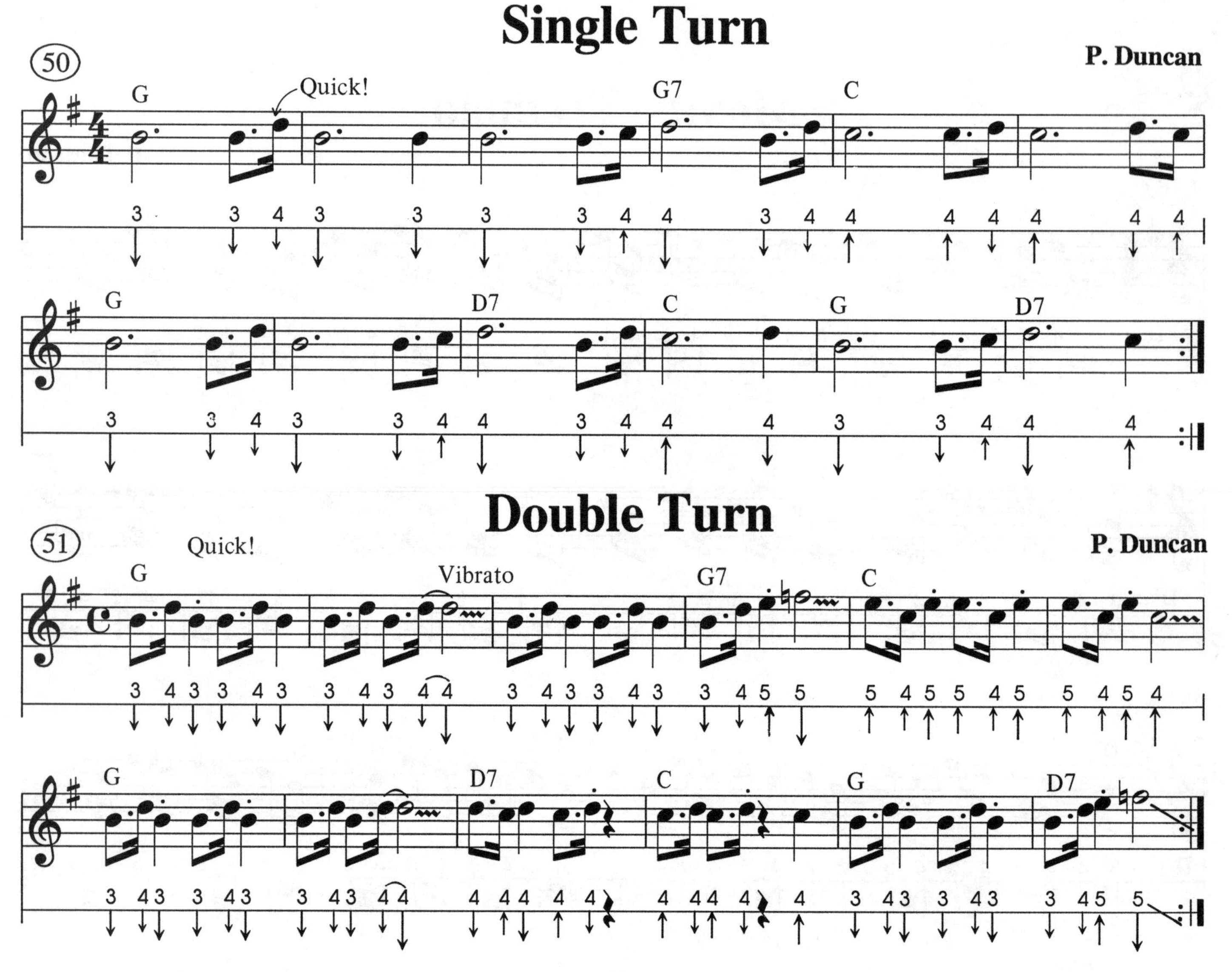

The "Articulated" Slide

Each tone is played separately, yet in a slide form. In this pattern, which is referred to as "pick-up" notes, start the first count in the next measure or section. You will need to start slowly and develop a quick speed, making sure you articulate each tone. Some will have three-note introductions, and others will use a four-note pick-up.

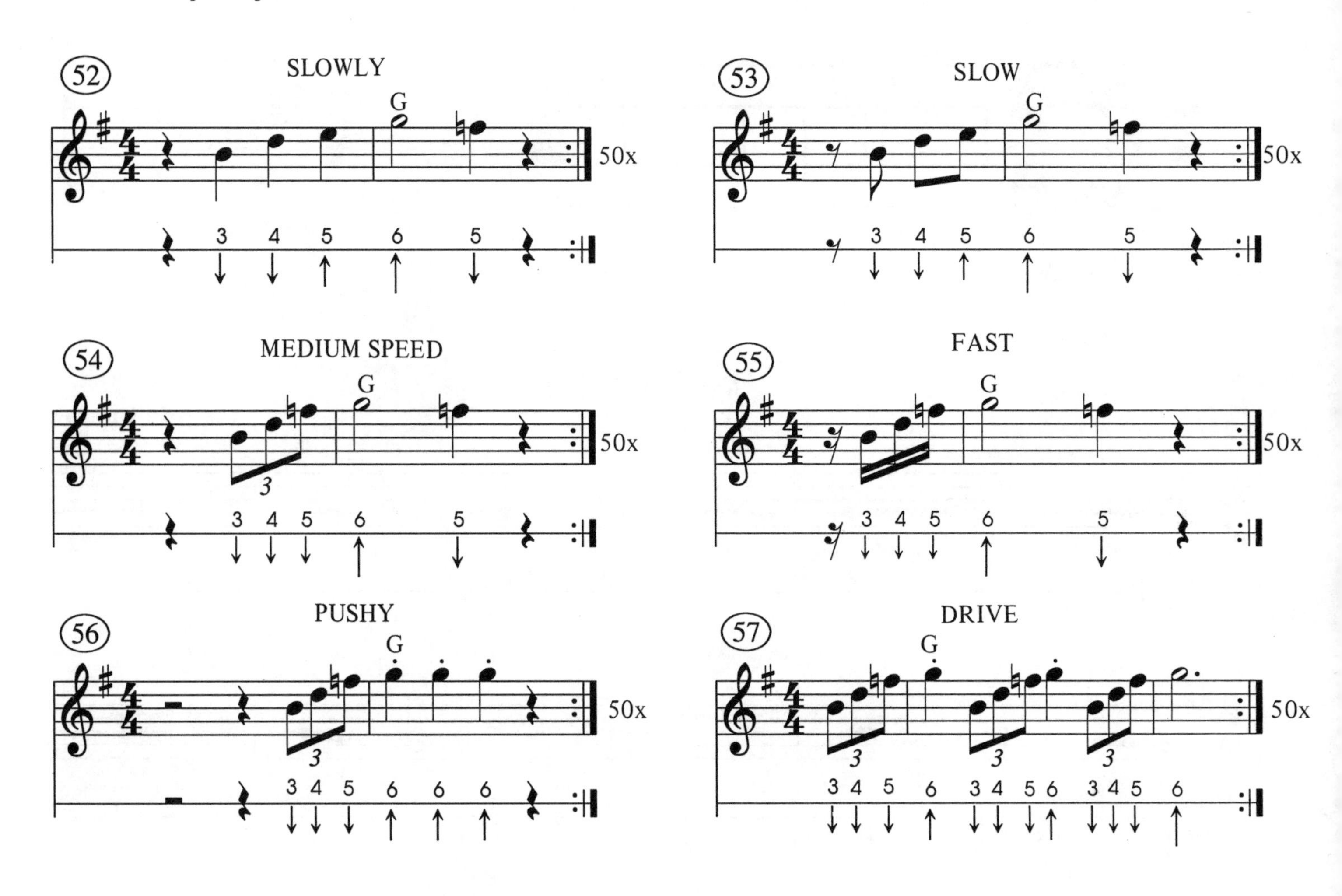

Pick-up Blues

P. Duncan

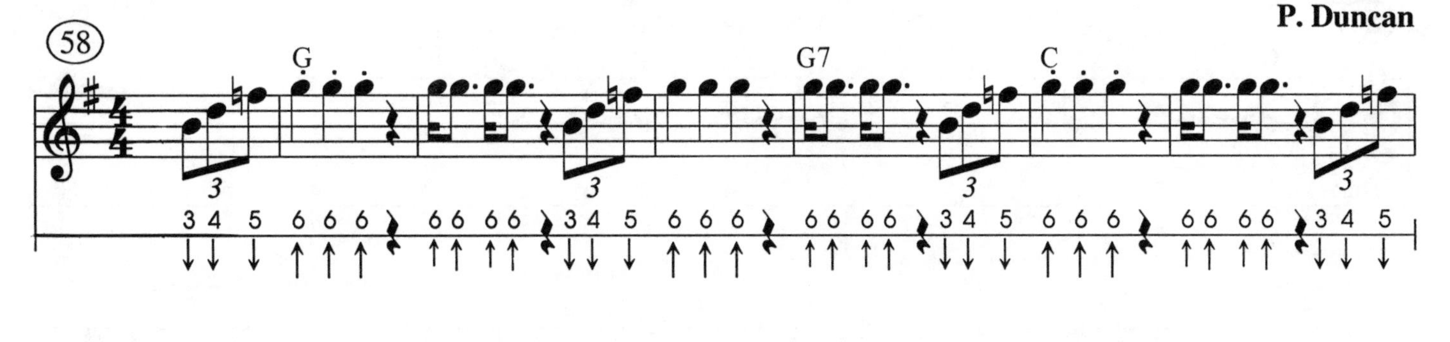

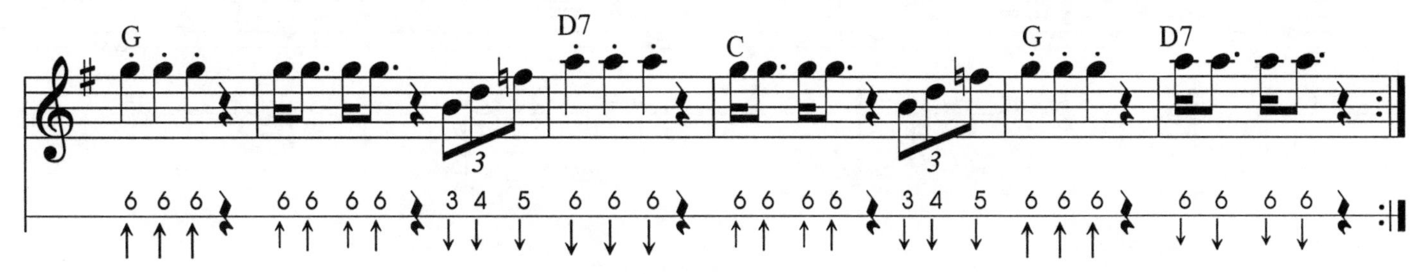

The "g" draw tone can be difficult to play — it seems to "choke" and not play, or play with a lot of air noise. However, after countless hours of playing, draw hole 2 will perform. In the meantime, it is possible to substitute hole 3; it is a "G" tone also. To perform hole 2, you will need to allow air to escape through the nose, relieving pressure. Play very gently at first, then increase the air supply as you practice.

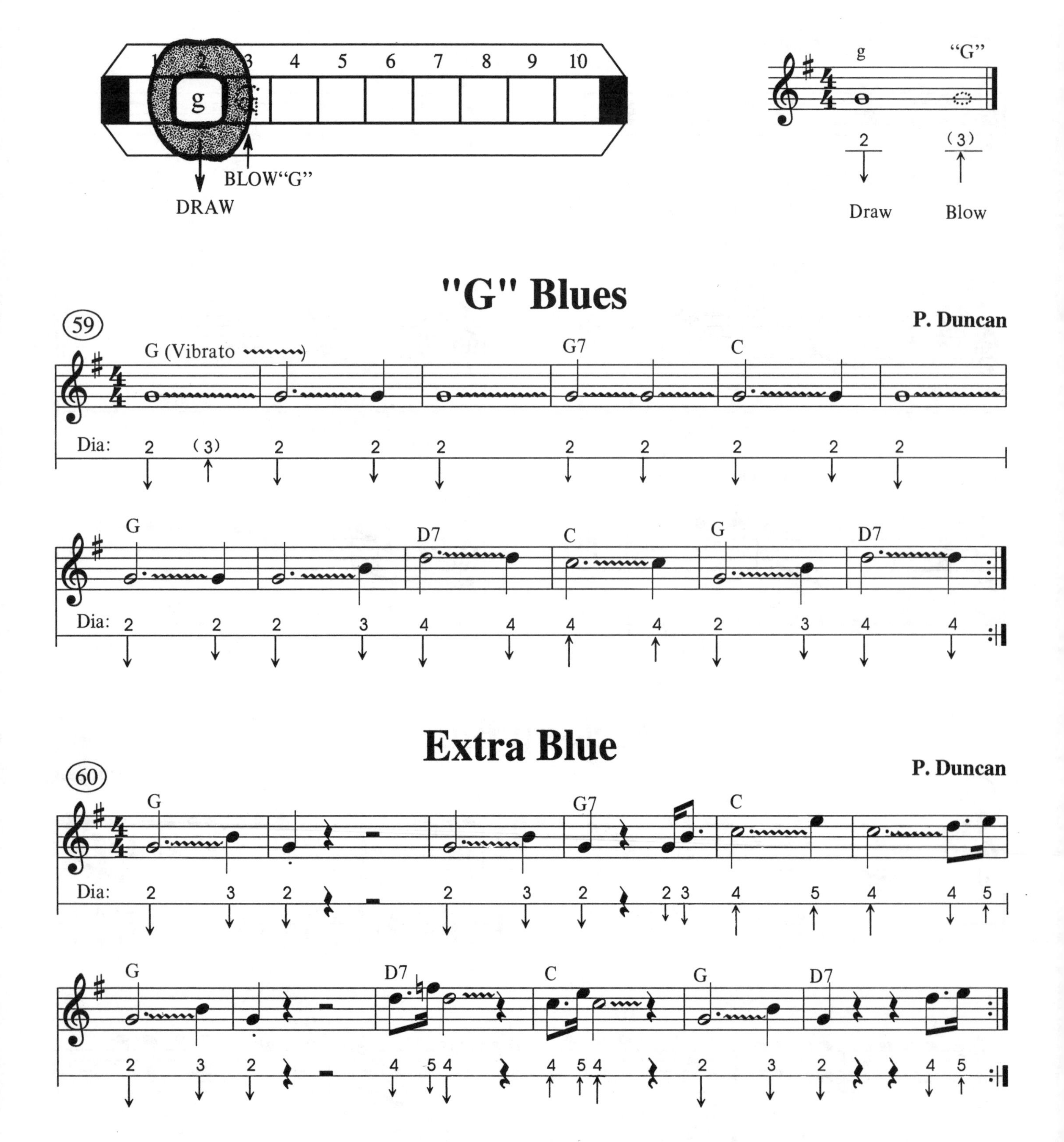

Lower End Tones

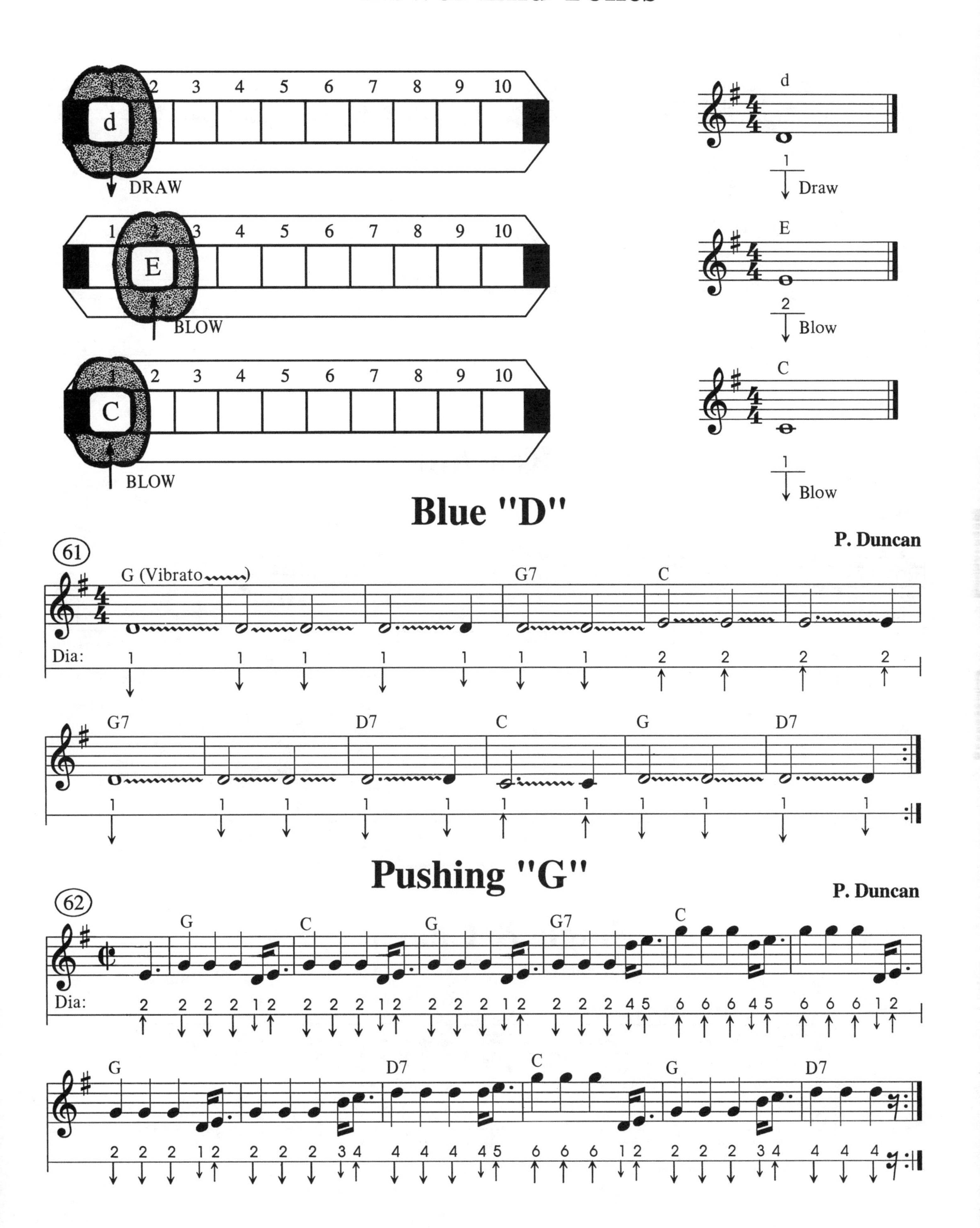

Target

P. Duncan

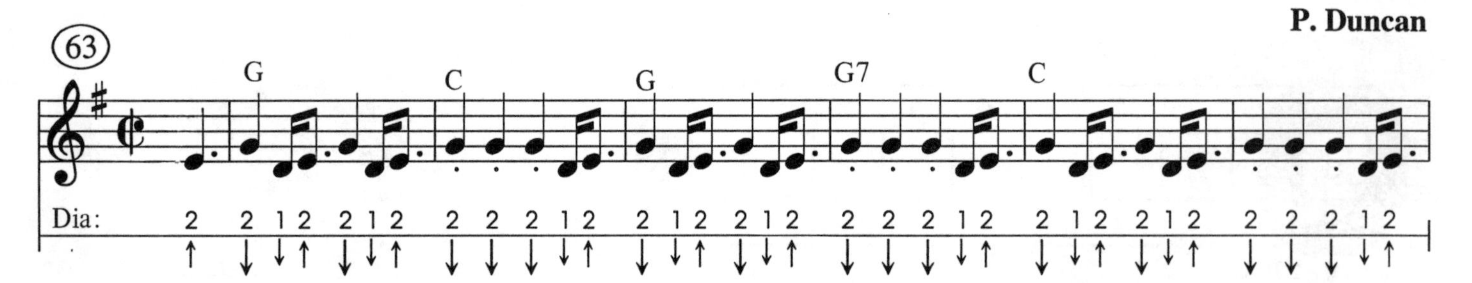

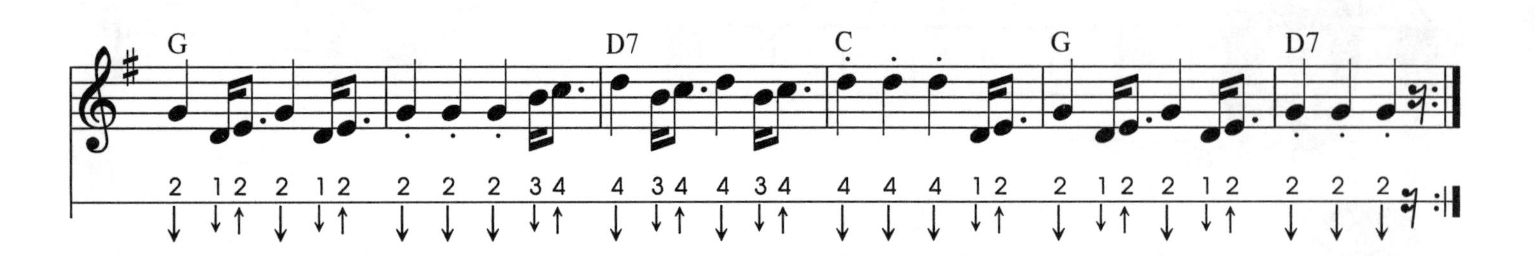

Reaching

P. Duncan

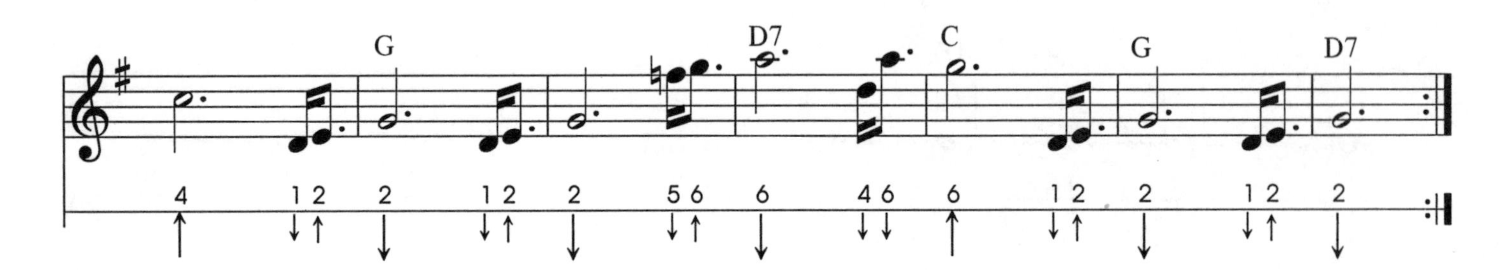

Single & Chord

P. Duncan

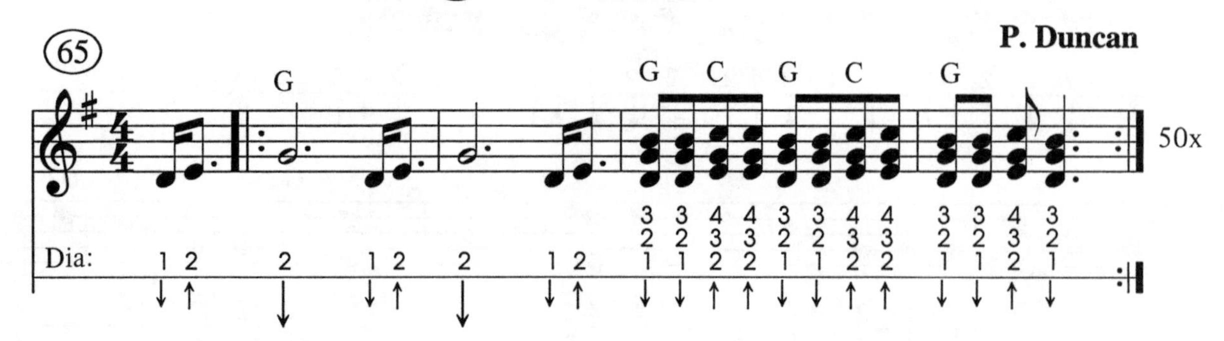

Rhythm Blues
66
P. Duncan
Swing
Dia:
67
50x
Dia:
Step It Up!
68
P. Duncan
Dia:

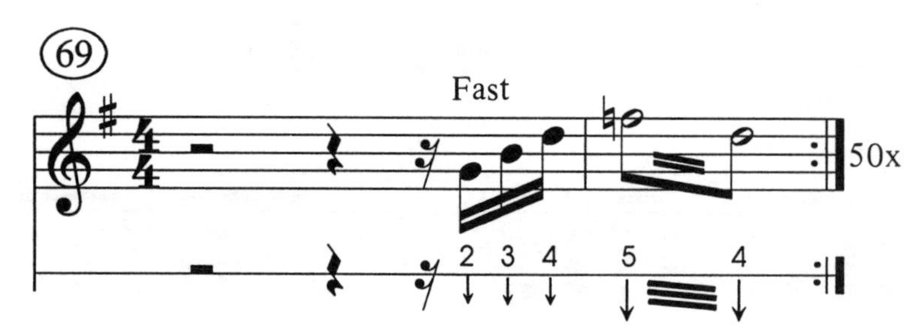
69
Fast
50x

Chicago Blues
70
P. Duncan
G (Tremolo)
G7
C
Dia:
G
D7
C
G
C
G
D7
Slide
Little Chicago
71
P. Duncan
G
G7
C
Slide
Dia:
(Tremolo)
G
D7
C
G
C
G
D7
Slide
Uptown Chicago
72
P. Duncan
G (Tremolo)
G7
C
Dia:
G (Tremolo)
D7
C
G
C
G
D7

73
Fast
Blow
Fast
Blow
50x
Dia:
Punch
P. Duncan
74
G
G7
C
Dia:
G
D7
C
G
D7
75
G
50x
Super Slide Blues
P. Duncan
76
G
Dia:
G7
C
G
D7
C
G
C
D7

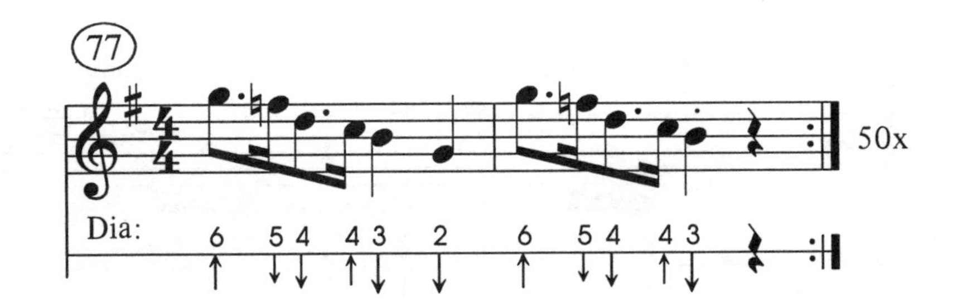

Down Blues

P. Duncan

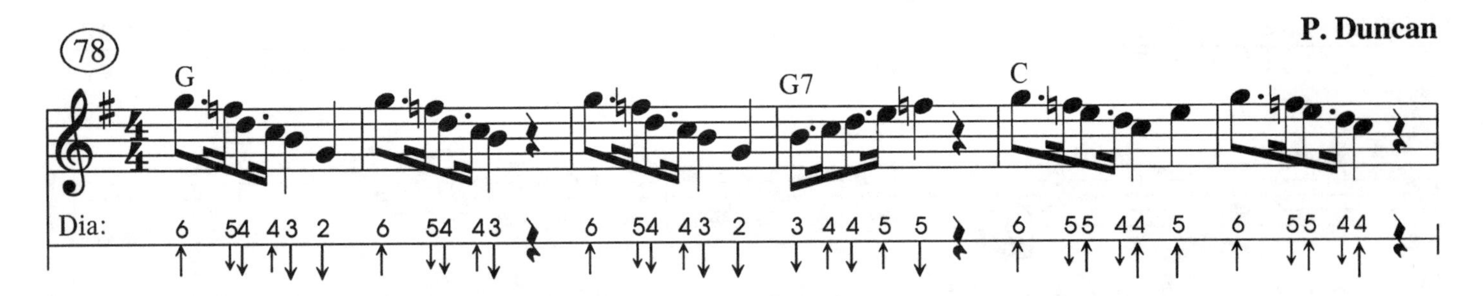

Boogie On Down

P. Duncan

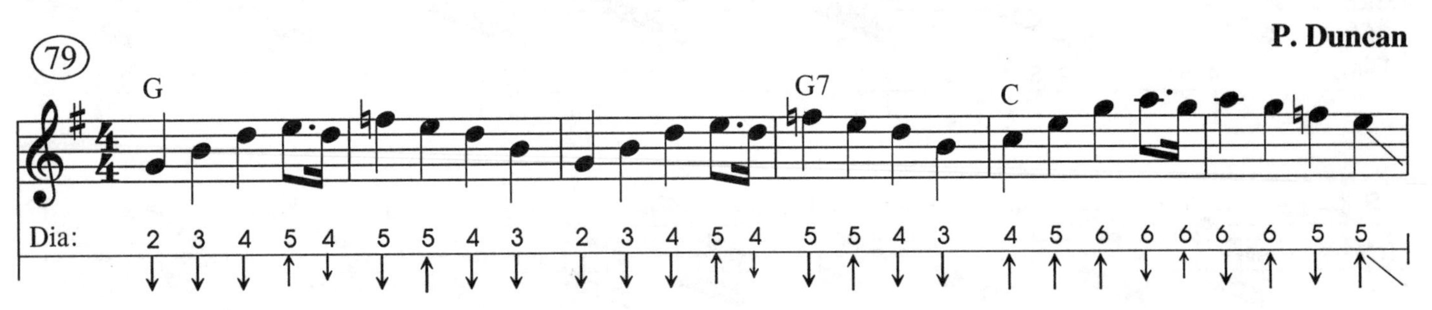

"Bending" Tones

Bending tones, making sharps and flats on the diatonic harmonica, is possible by slowing the speed of the vibrating reed. This is done by added air pressure to the chamber and the reed, causing the reed to slow down its number of vibrations per second.

"How To"

To physically achieve this, one must remember to continue to practice. Lips and mouth muscles need to be strengthened; therefore, some practice and persistence will be necessary.

Sometimes using a lower-pitched harmonica, like a "B flat" or "A" harmonica, can help the process.

When sucking or drawing air through holes 1, 2, 3, 4, or 6, drop your jaw a little and the tip of your tongue. This will arch your tongue in the middle of your mouth and make the air dart down to the stomach.

First play hole 1 draw, bending to "D flat." Next move to hole 4 and bend to "D flat," then to hole 6 for "A flat." Now move to hole 3. This hole will bend a whole step to the "A" tone. "B flat" is there somewhere in between. Lastly, move to hole 2 and again bend a whole step to "F." There is also an "F sharp" in between. Remember, you must purse or pucker your lips.

As you work for the "bent" or flat tones, continue to practice to achieve the passages that do not require bent tones. The next section will introduce flatted tones, such as the flat 5th ("D flat") and the flat 3rd ("B flat").

Air Flow

By changing the flow of the air and the shape of the mouth cavity, the tone can be changed to a lower pitch when you draw air through the harmonica. This is the way to lower or flat a tone on the harmonica, called *bending*. By changing the flow of the air (see illustration below), you can affect the pitch of the reed.

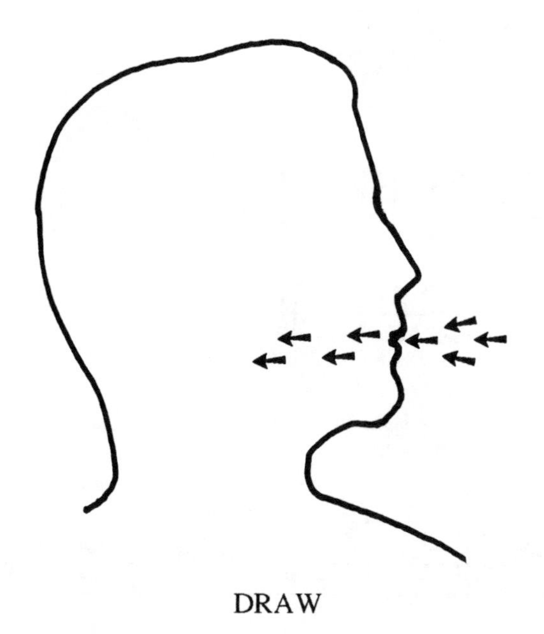

DRAW

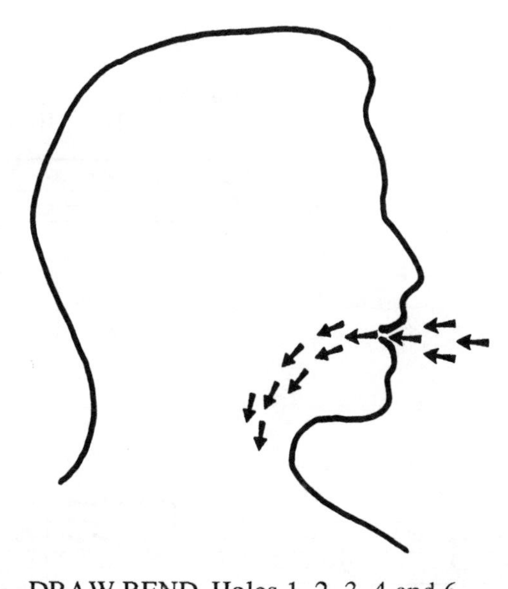

DRAW BEND Holes 1, 2, 3, 4 and 6

The circled number means to lower the pitch one half step, such as "D" to "D flat" and "A" to "A flat." The curved or bent arrow indicates bending the sound.

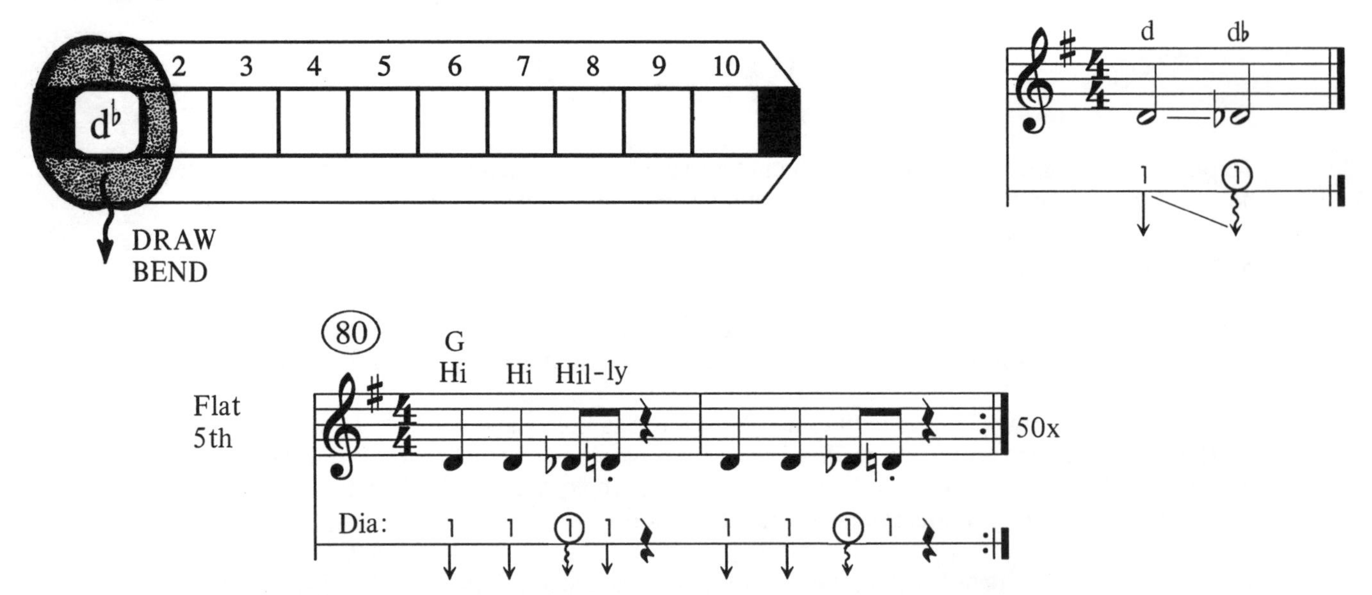

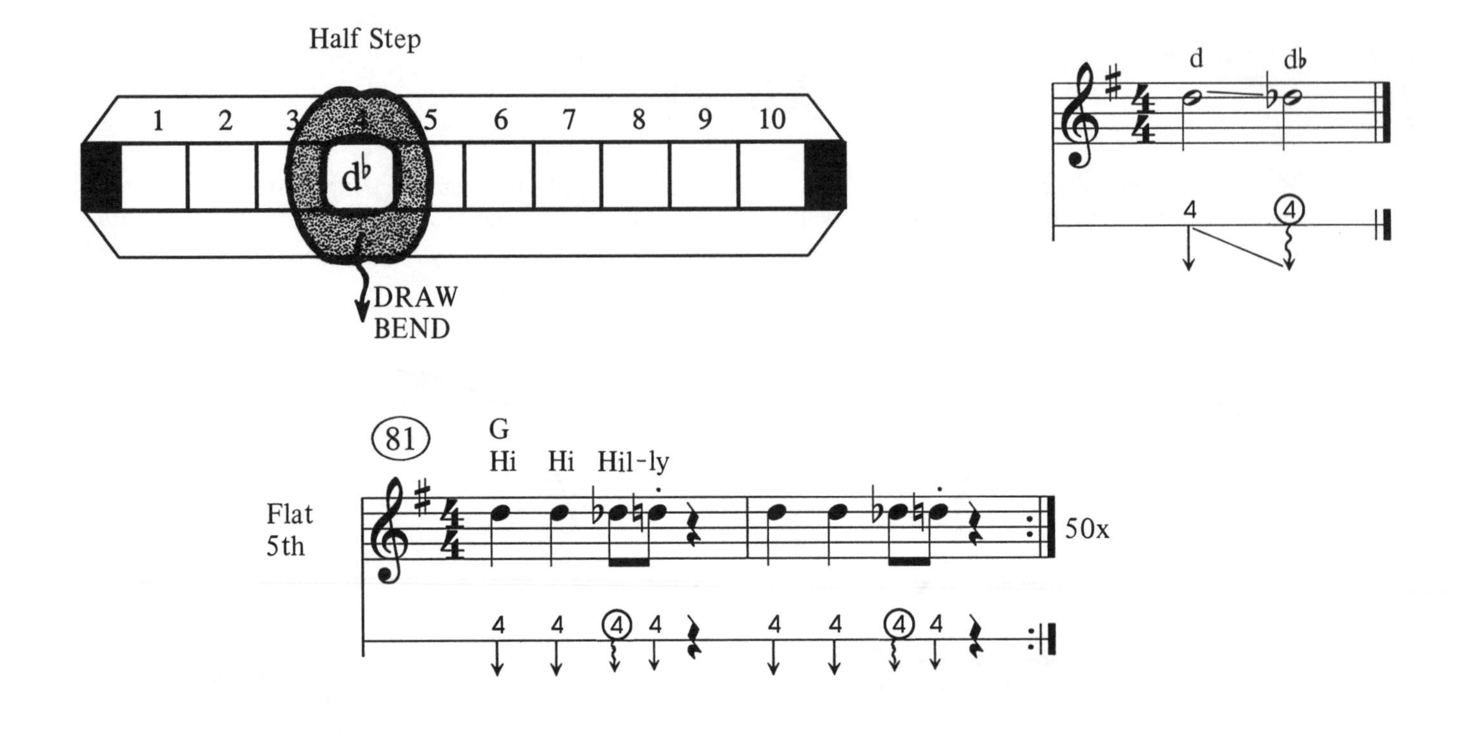

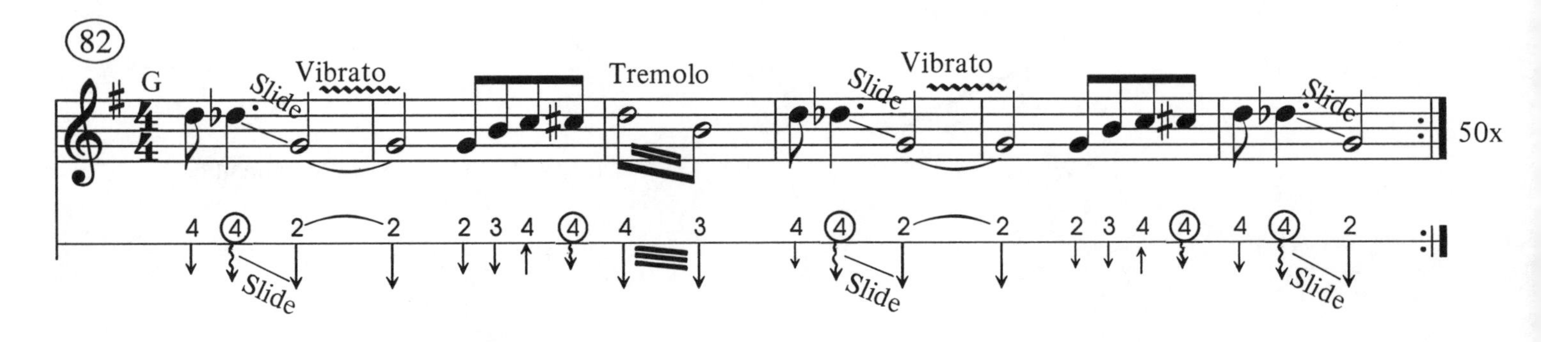

After playing the single hole 2, draw, expand your mouth on holes 1, 2, and 3, draw. Then blow 1, 2, and 3. Last, draw again on holes 1, 2, and 3, then back to the single-tone "G" hole 2, draw, to start over. At the end of the second time, move to hole 4 and draw, then bend and slide to hole 2, draw, and start the pattern again.

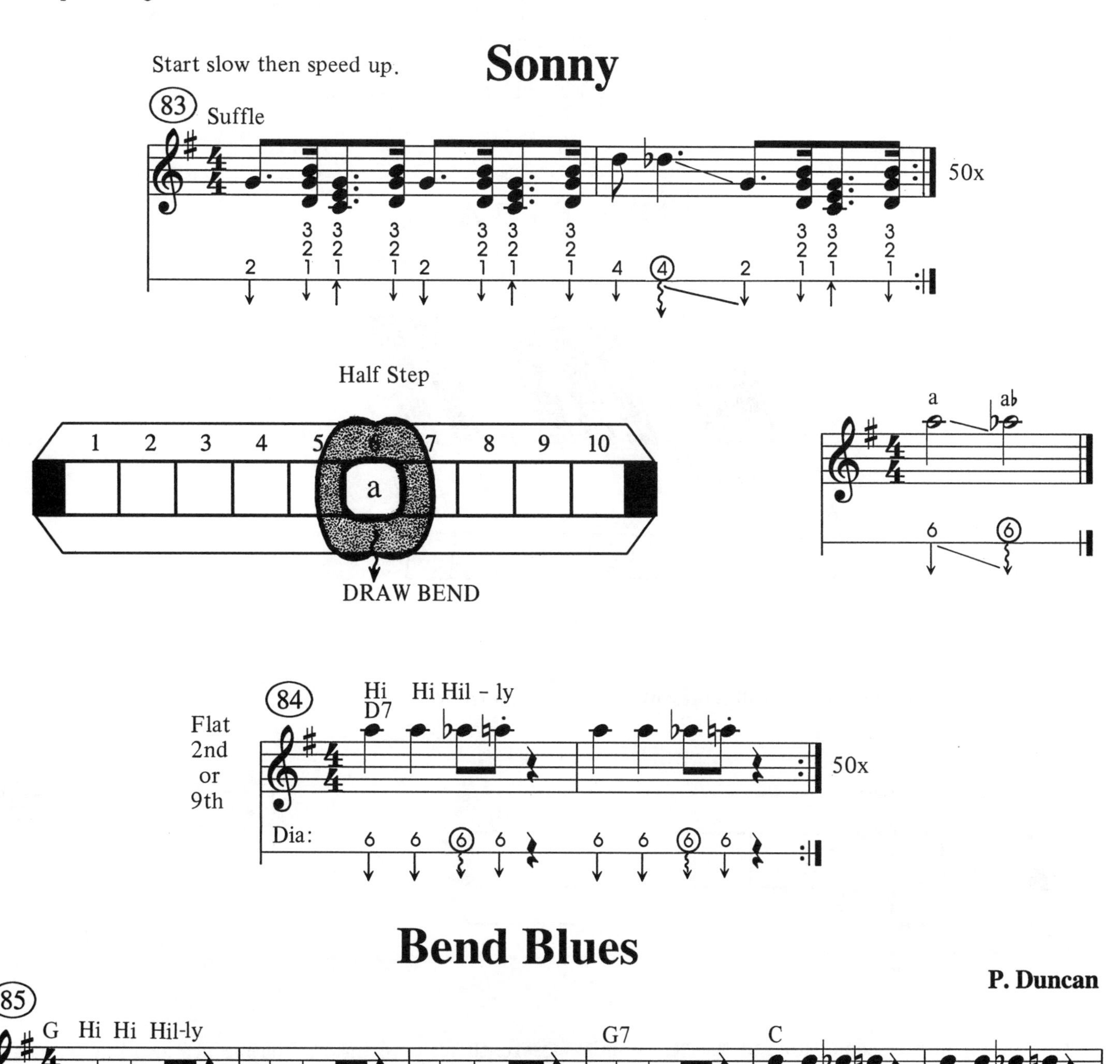

"B" To "A"

When working with hole 3, the bend will naturally be deeper, like "B" to "A," not "B" to "B flat." "B flat" is bent a little, and "A" is bent more. It will take ear training to know and hear the difference. Use a piano or guitar to hear the difference between a whole step and a half step. "B" to "A" is the whole step, and "B" to "B flat" is the half step. First we will examine the bent "A."

Notice: There is an "A flat" in bend hole 3, but it is not really used as a single note.

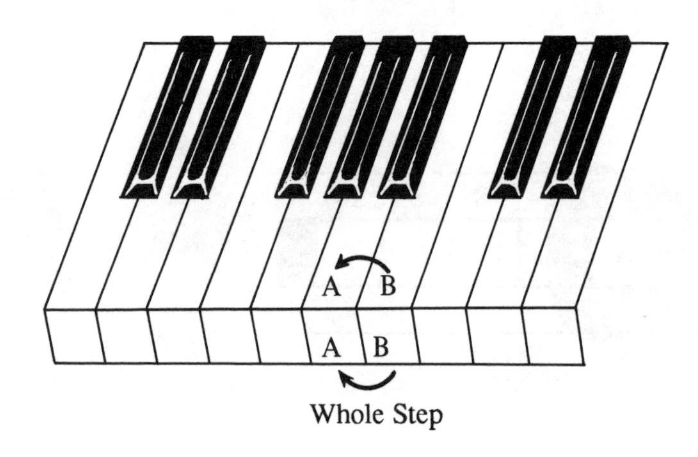

The square around the number will represent the whole step to "A".

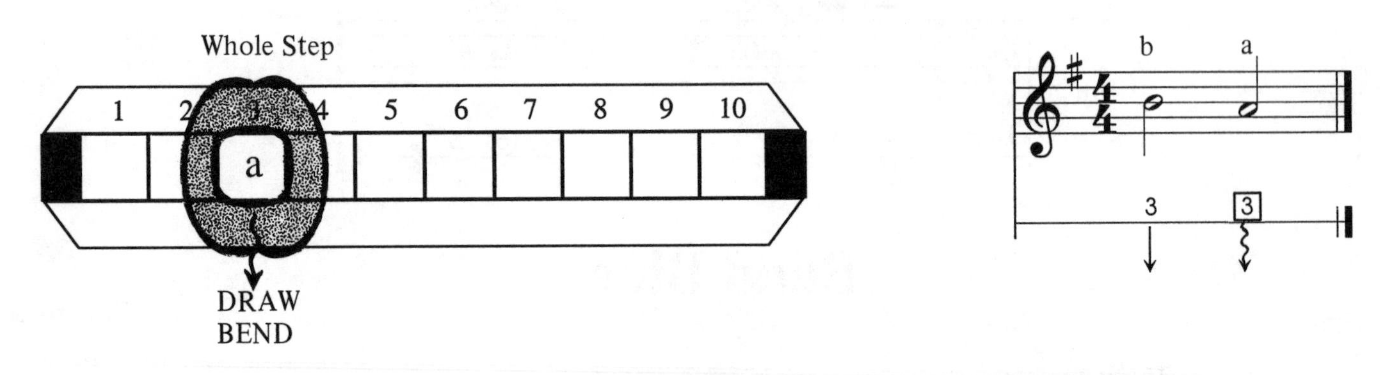

This gives you the second tone of the "G" dominant seventh scale on the "C" harmonica also known as a mixolydian scale.

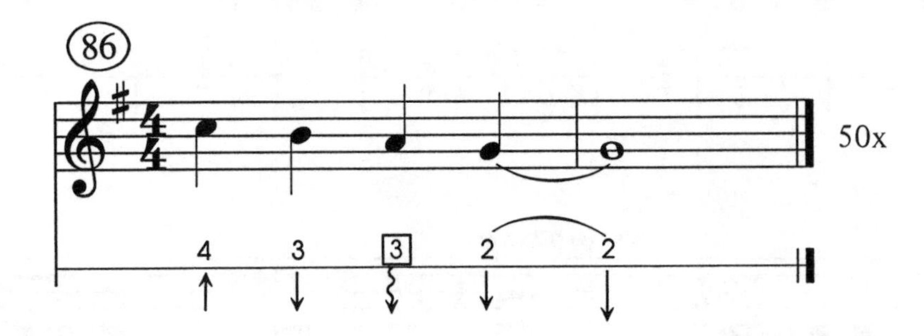

"G" Dominant Scale
Mixolydian Scale

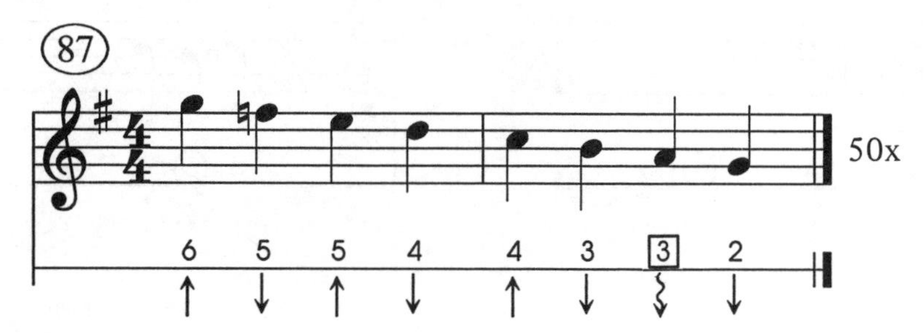

To help with ear training try to play a portion of "Mary Had a Little Lamb". The second tone requires the "A" bent tone on hole three (3).

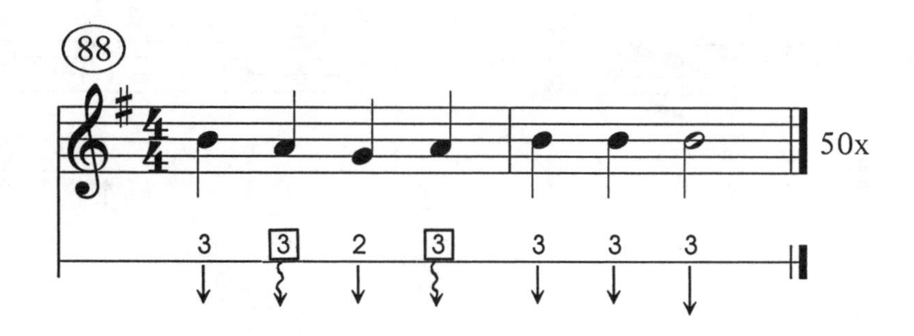

"B" To "B Flat"

"B flat" will give a "dirty" or gravel-type sound. In blues, it gives us the not-quite-right feeling. Therefore, being not quite right on pitch in this case is okay.

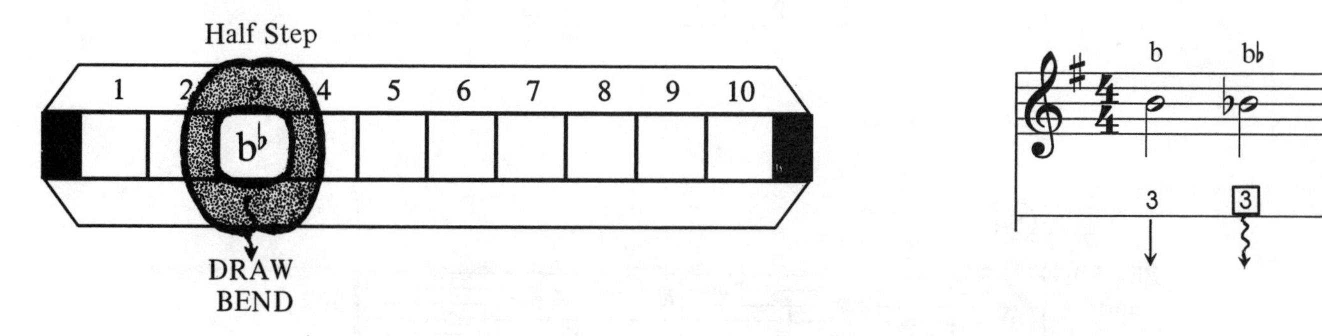

Ear training will be necessary to hear the exact pitch required for the "B flat" tone. This is necessary from hole 4 "C" to "B flat," another whole step. However, "B" to "B flat" is also still necessary to hear. Using the keyboard (piano) will help.

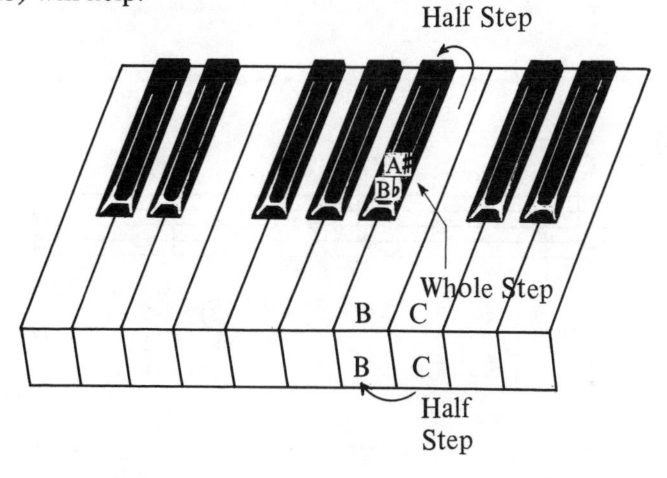

"B Flat" Ear Training

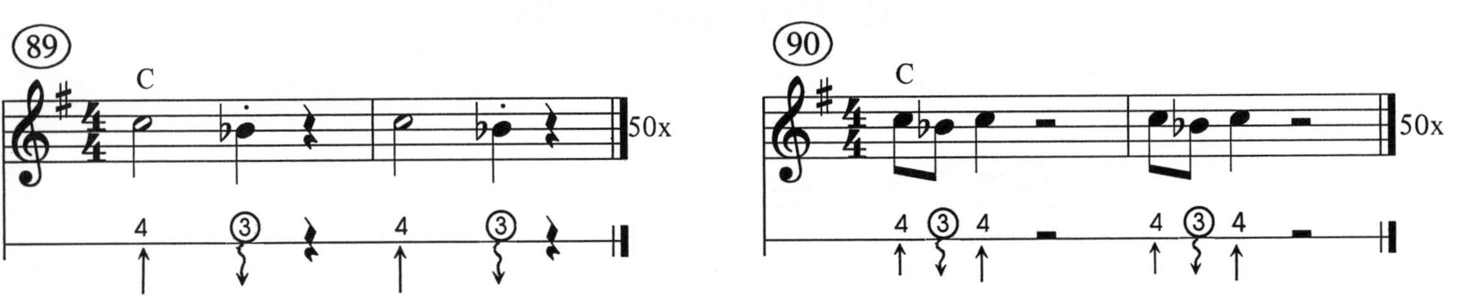

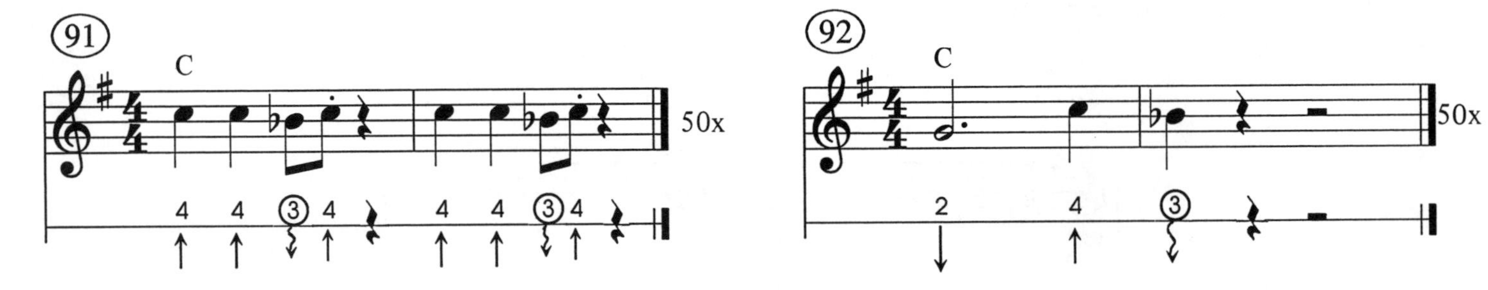

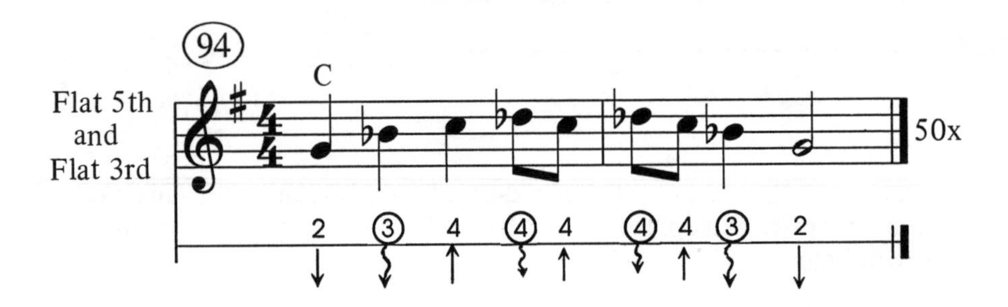

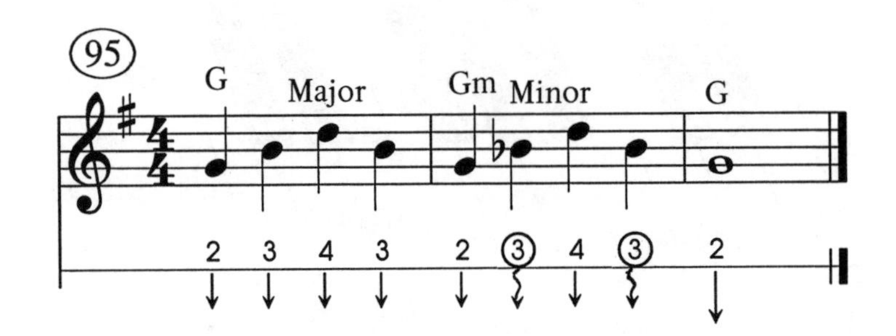

Easy Blues Scale

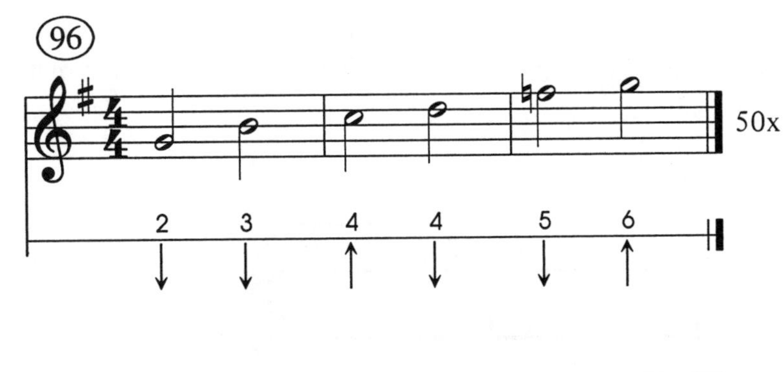

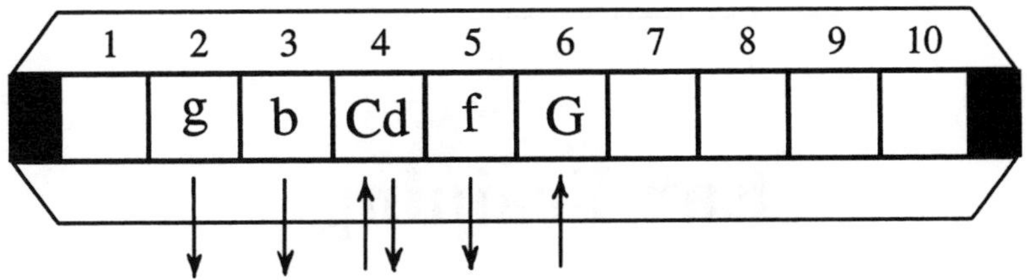

Actual Blues Scale

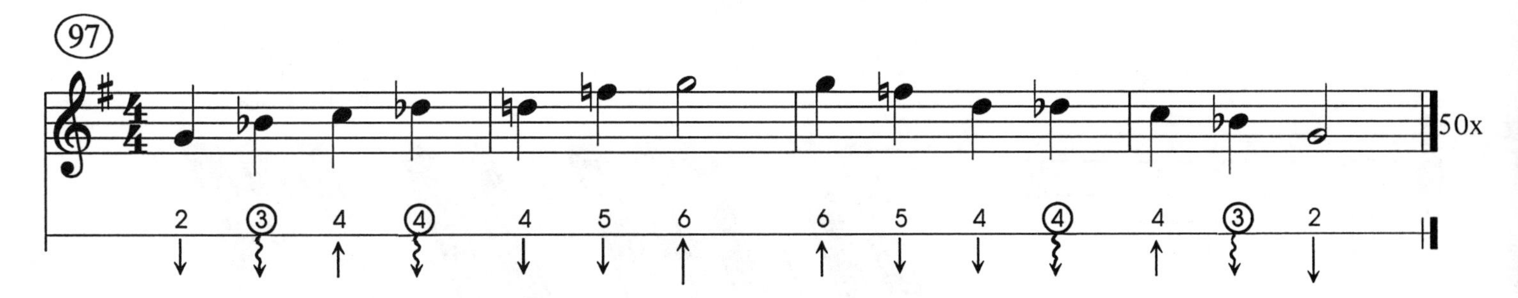

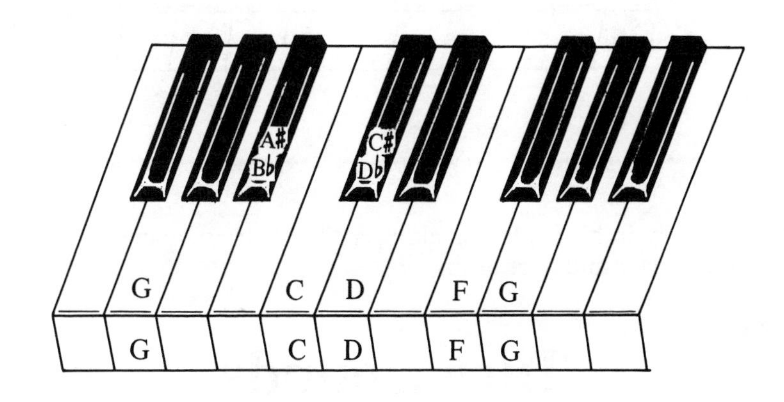

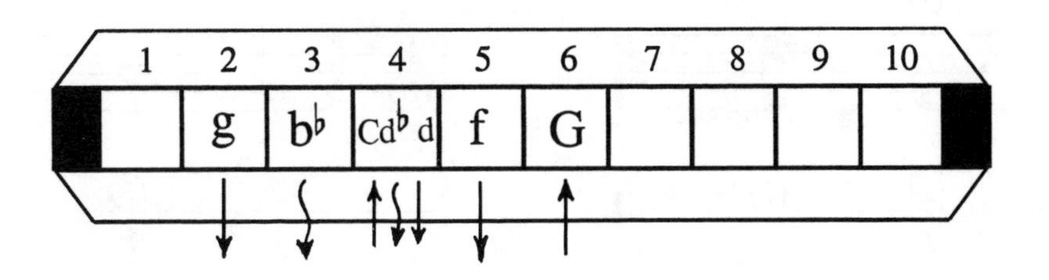

"G" To "F"

Hole 2, like hole three draw, bending a lower tone, like "G" to "F" is more natural than bending a little, like "G" to "F sharp."

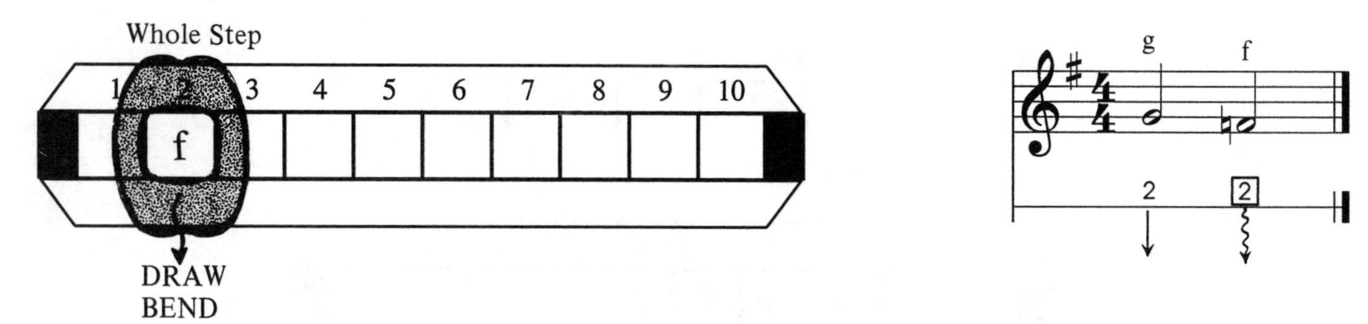

Ear Training

For ear training purposes, hole two bent is the same pitch as hole five draw.

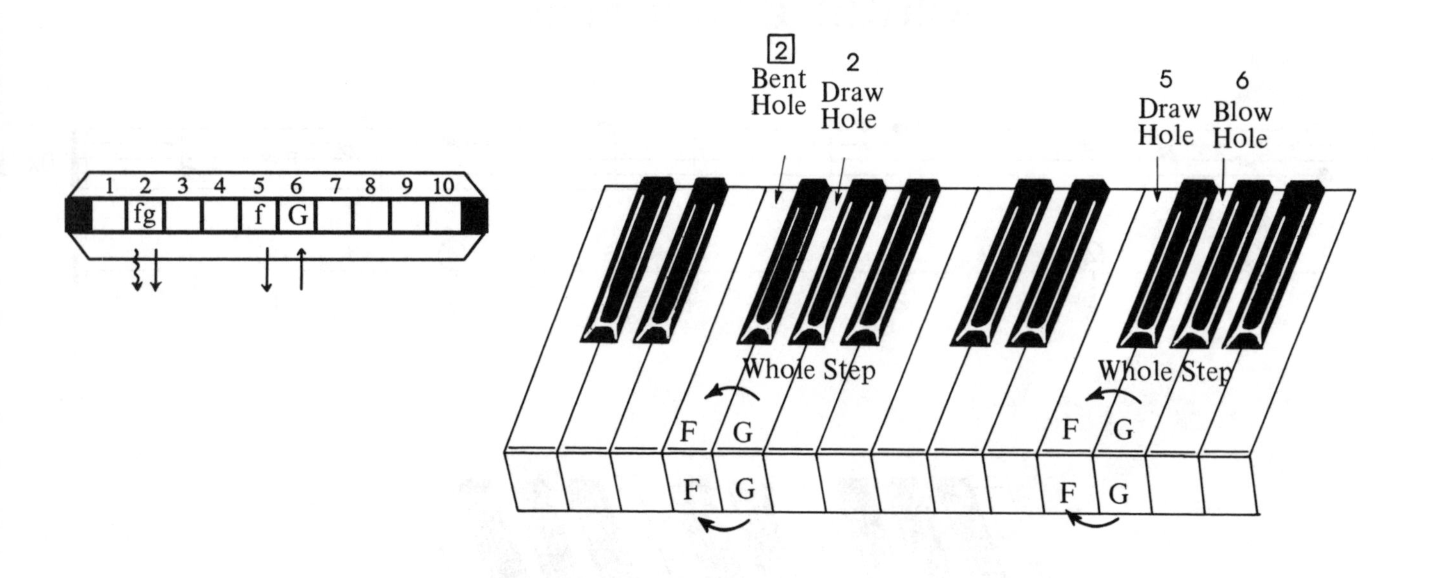

This tone is used continuously in blues playing along with the draw hole 1 "D". This creates a "Turnaround", to be able to start the piece over and over again.

Turnarounds

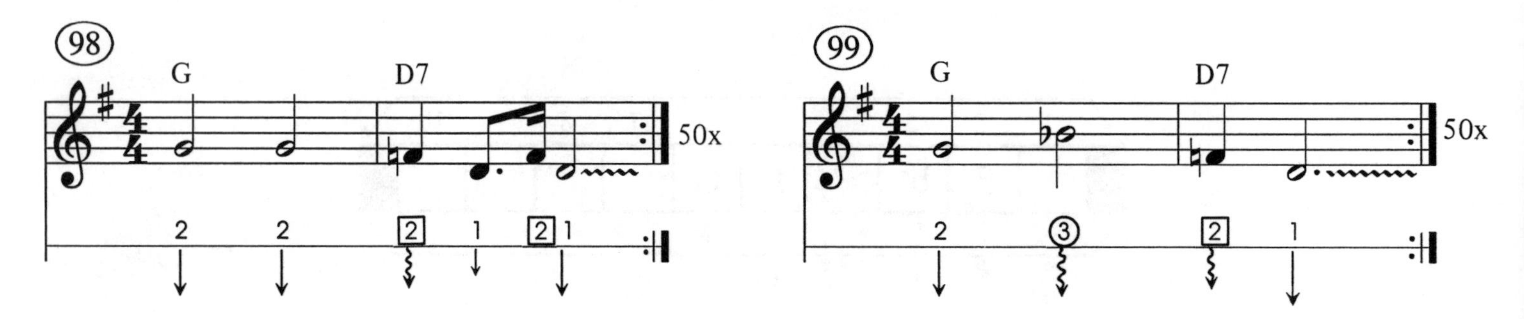

More Turnarounds

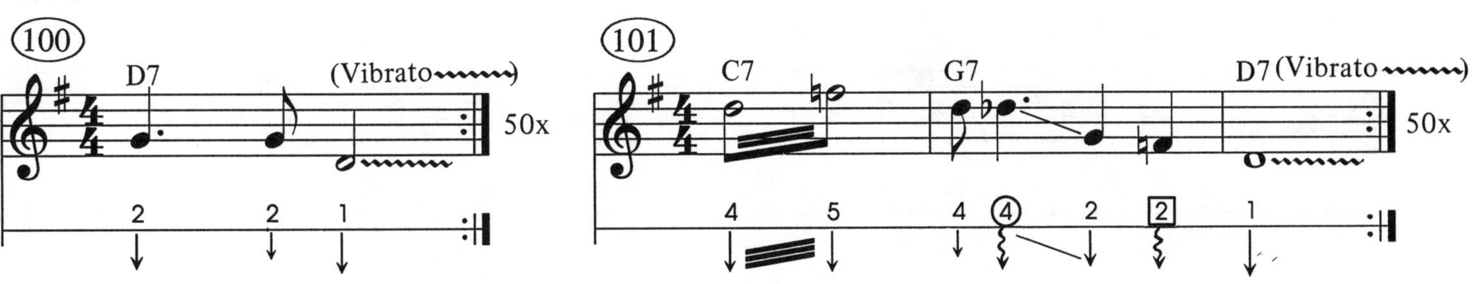

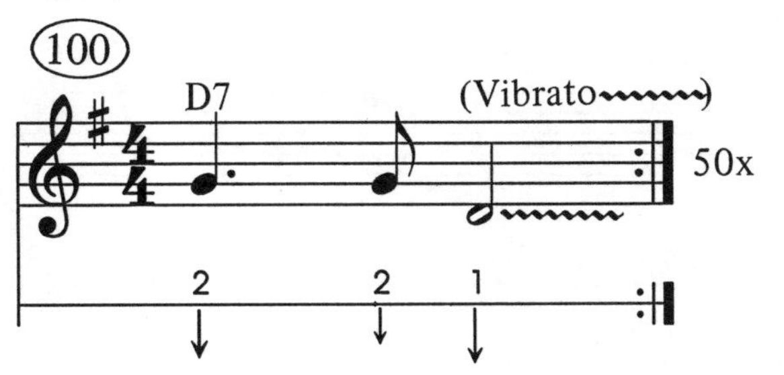

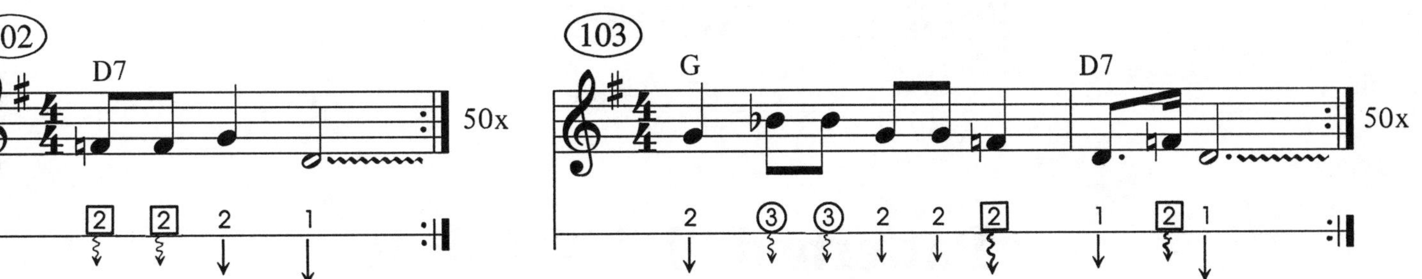

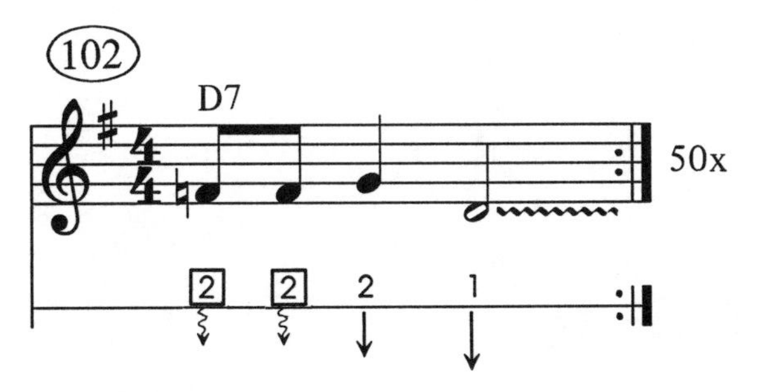

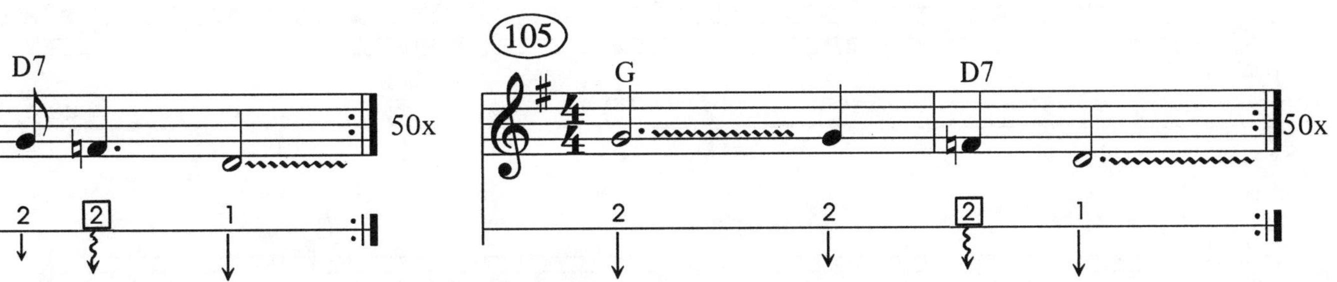

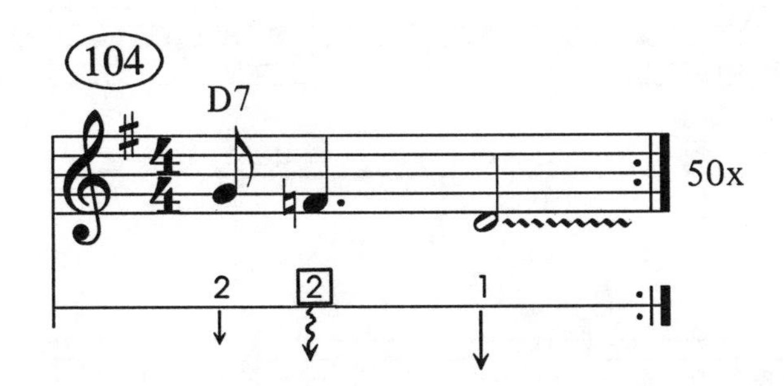

Other Turnarounds

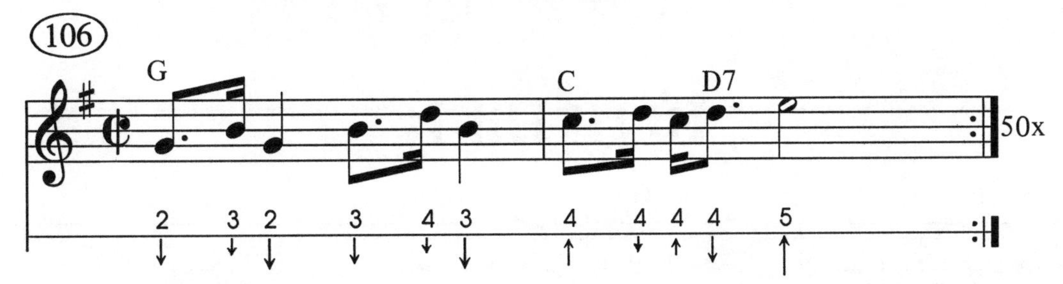

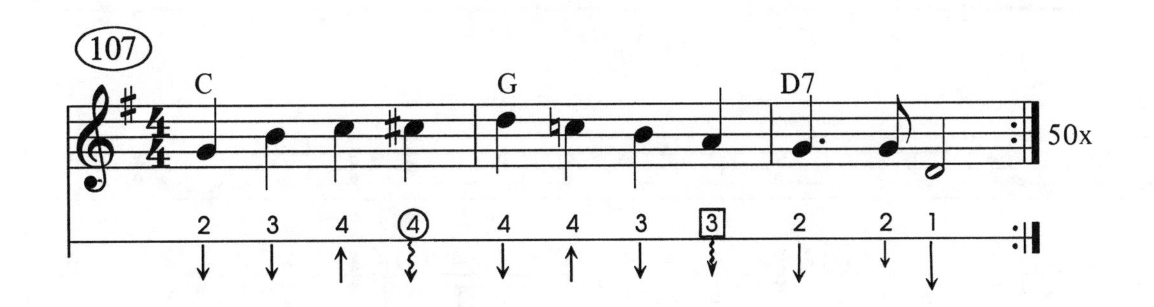

More "F" Natural

Patterned "F" Naturals

Come On
112
P. Duncan
G C G G7 C
Dia:
G D7 C G D7
Moving On
113
P. Duncan
G C G G7 C
Dia:
G D7 C G D7
Really Real
114
P. Duncan
G C G G7 C
Dia:
G D7 C G D7

Hil-ly Hi
115
P. Duncan
G
Hil-ly Hi
G7
C
Dia:
D7
Ho-o Hi Hi
116
P. Duncan
Ho-o
Hi
Hi
Ho Hi
117
P. Duncan
Ho
Hi

P. Duncan

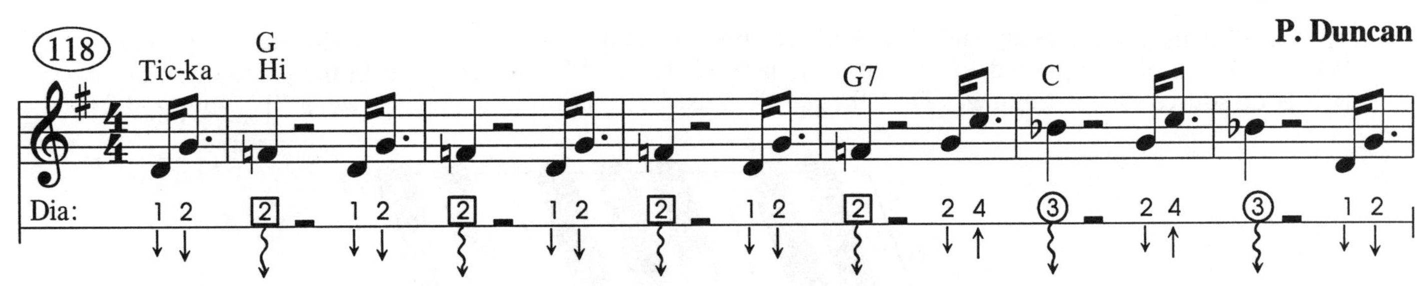

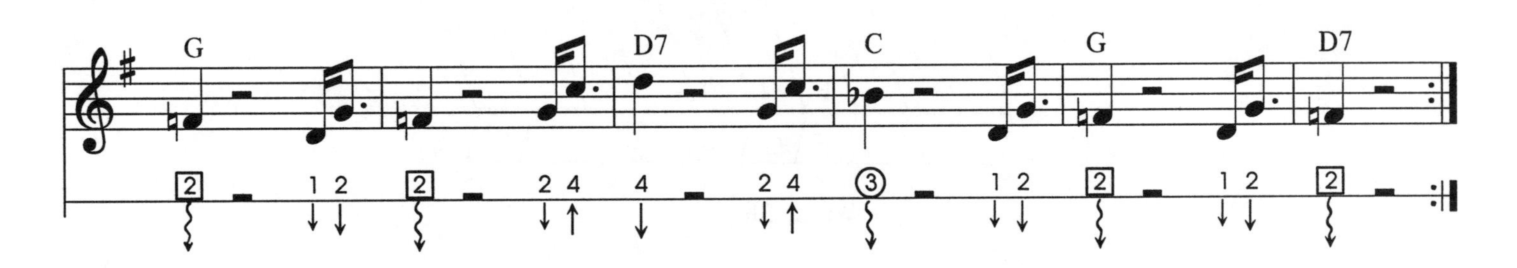

Hi Hi Hi Hi Hil-ly Hi Ho

P. Duncan

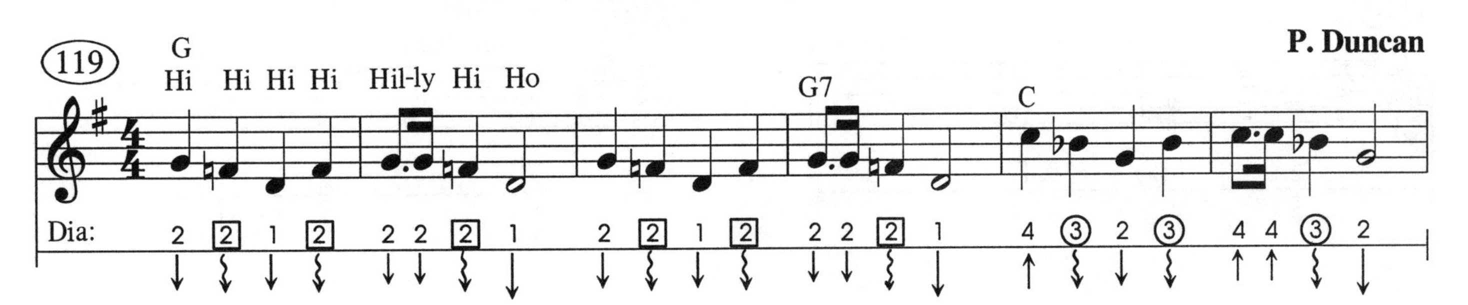

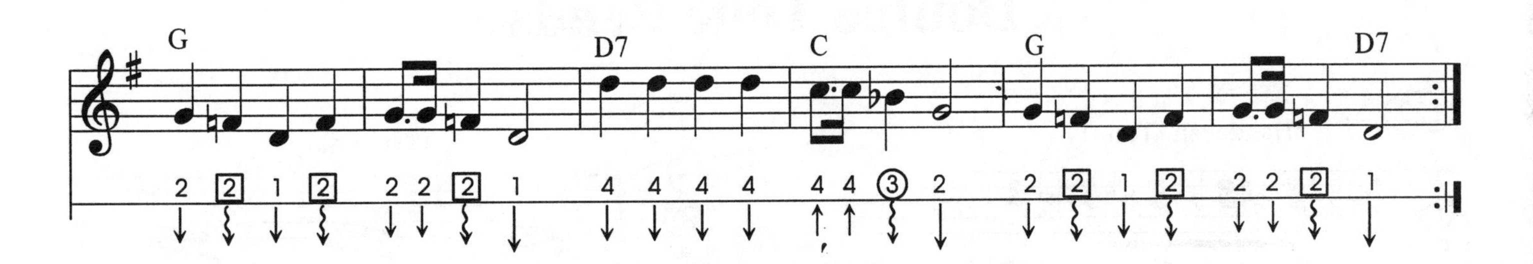

"G" to "f sharp"

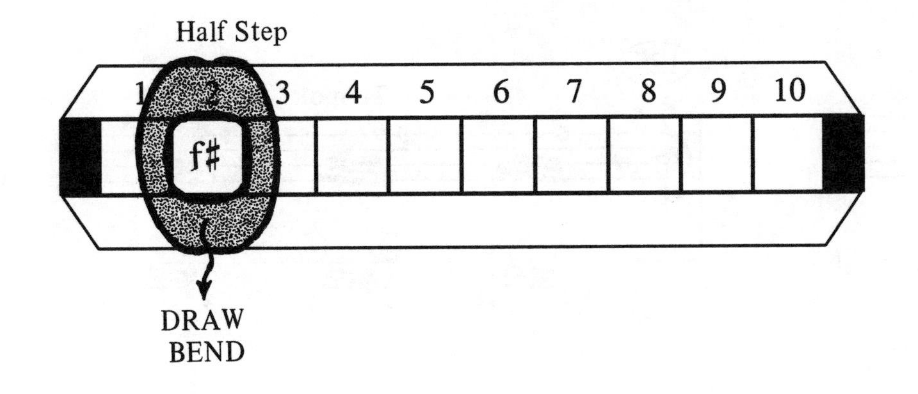

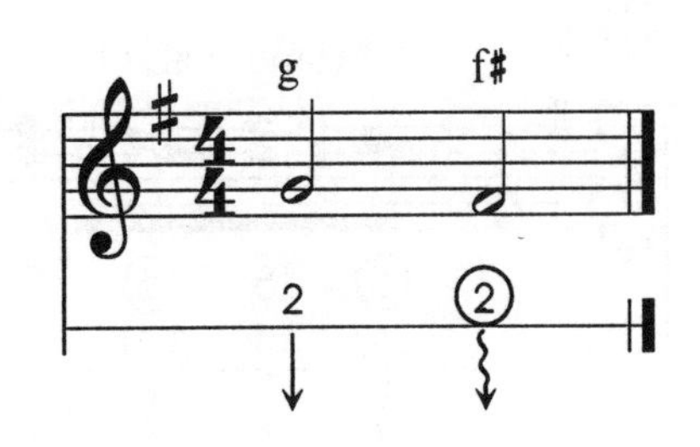

"F sharp" is used for playing melody. With ear training you will be able to hear this half step bent "G" to "F sharp" as opposed to the whole step bent "G" to "F natural". Again the piano or guitar is a good source for ear training. This "F sharp" is used as a chromatic step between "F" and "G".

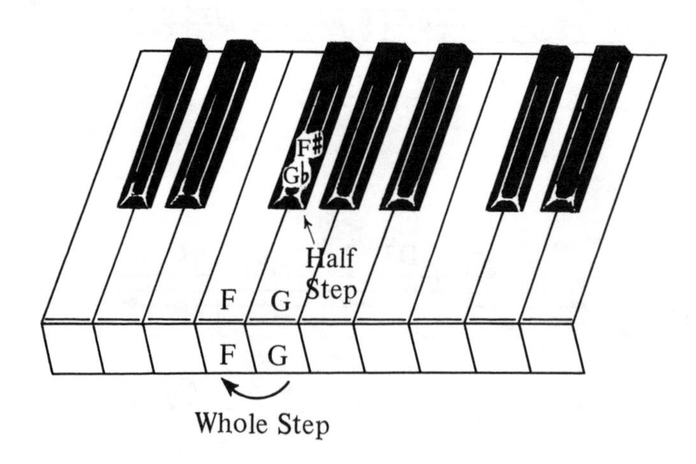

Endings

*Hand wah: open the hand suddenly, but on purpose.

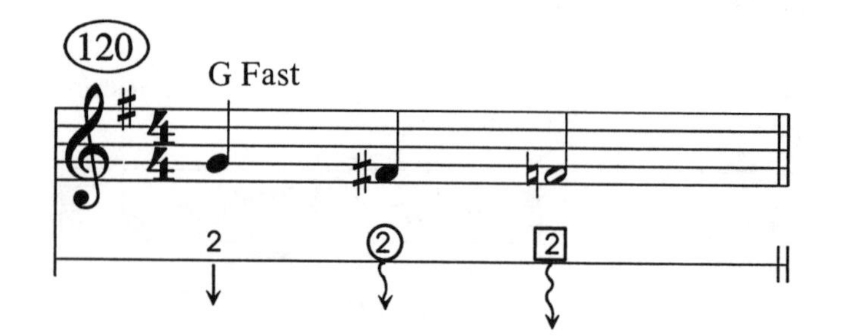

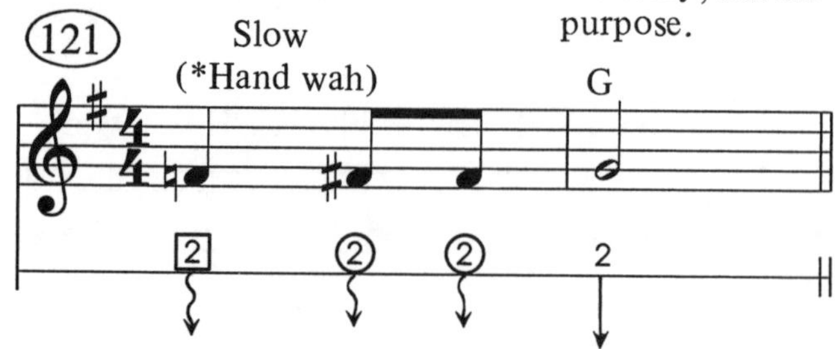

Double Tone Bends

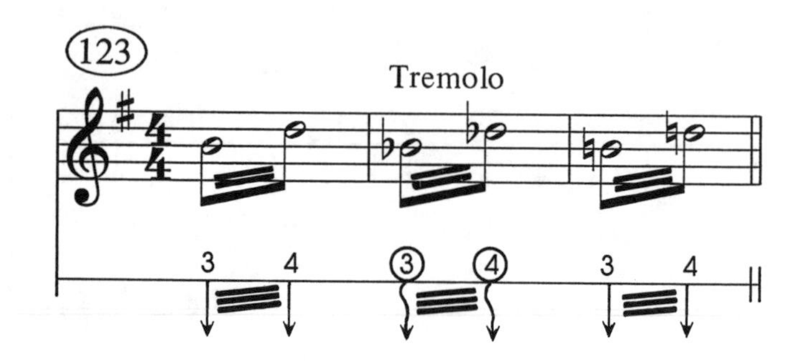

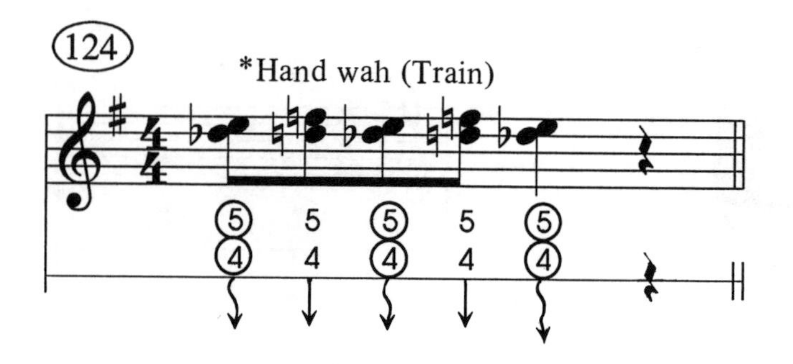

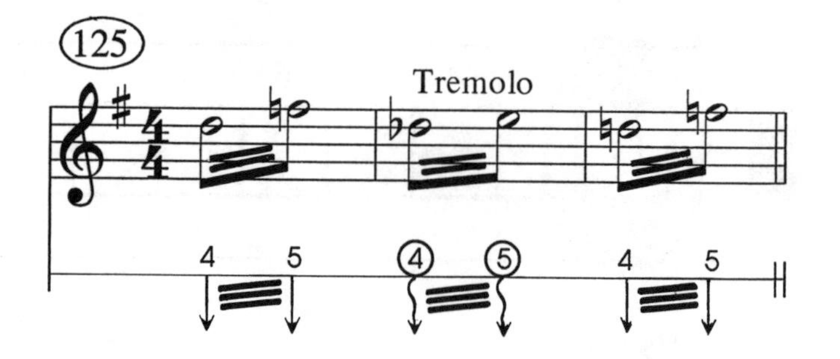

Twelve Bar Tremolo

Shake your head like saying "No." Or you may move the harmonica back and forth. The most important thing is to be steady, even, and relaxed. It is best to move the harmonica or your head to the rhythm of the song. This way you will not get lost in between the beats. This is an acquired skill, so keep playing!!!

Feelin'

128
P. Duncan
Dia:
Slide
Layed Back
129
P. Duncan
Blue Nat
130
P. Duncan
Dia:

Octave Playing

This technique requires the use of the tongue, blocking unwanted holes. The air will move out and in the corners of your mouth.

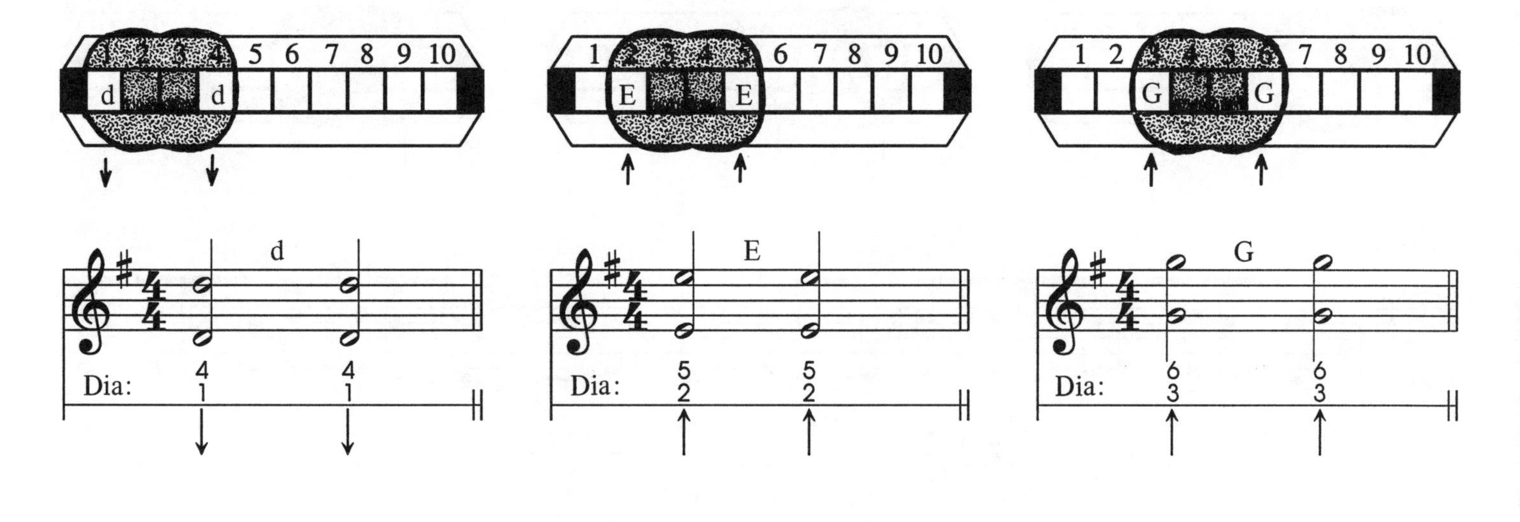

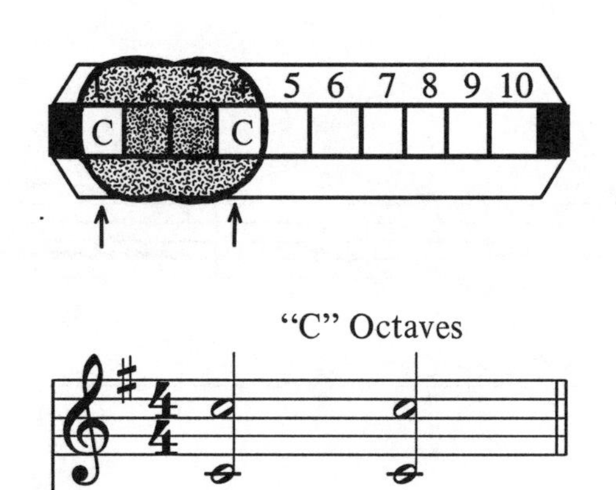

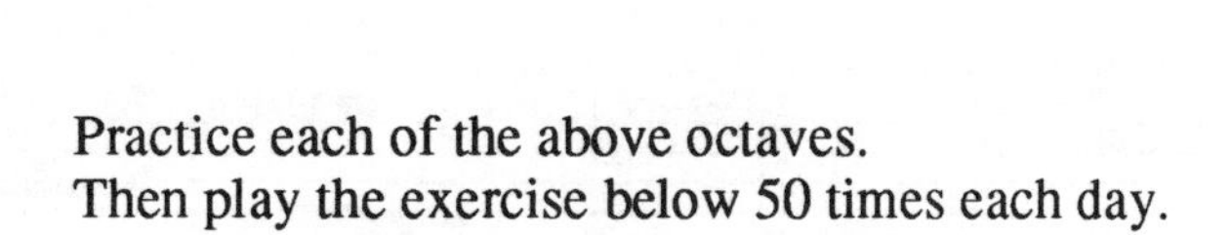

Practice each of the above octaves.
Then play the exercise below 50 times each day.

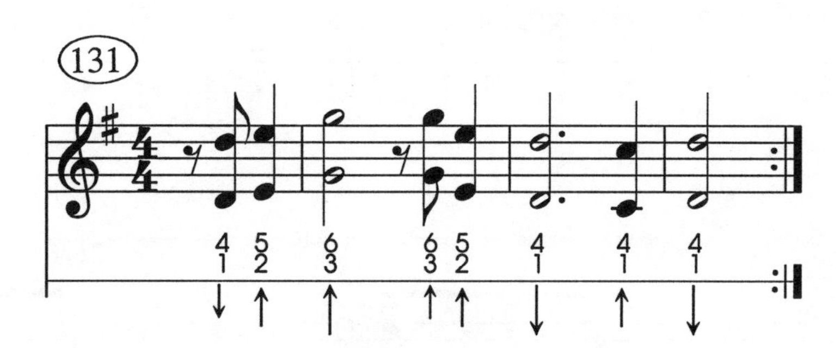

Octave playing can be done on the chromatic.
However, you need to open your mouth wider.

Octave Shuffle
(Diatonic only)

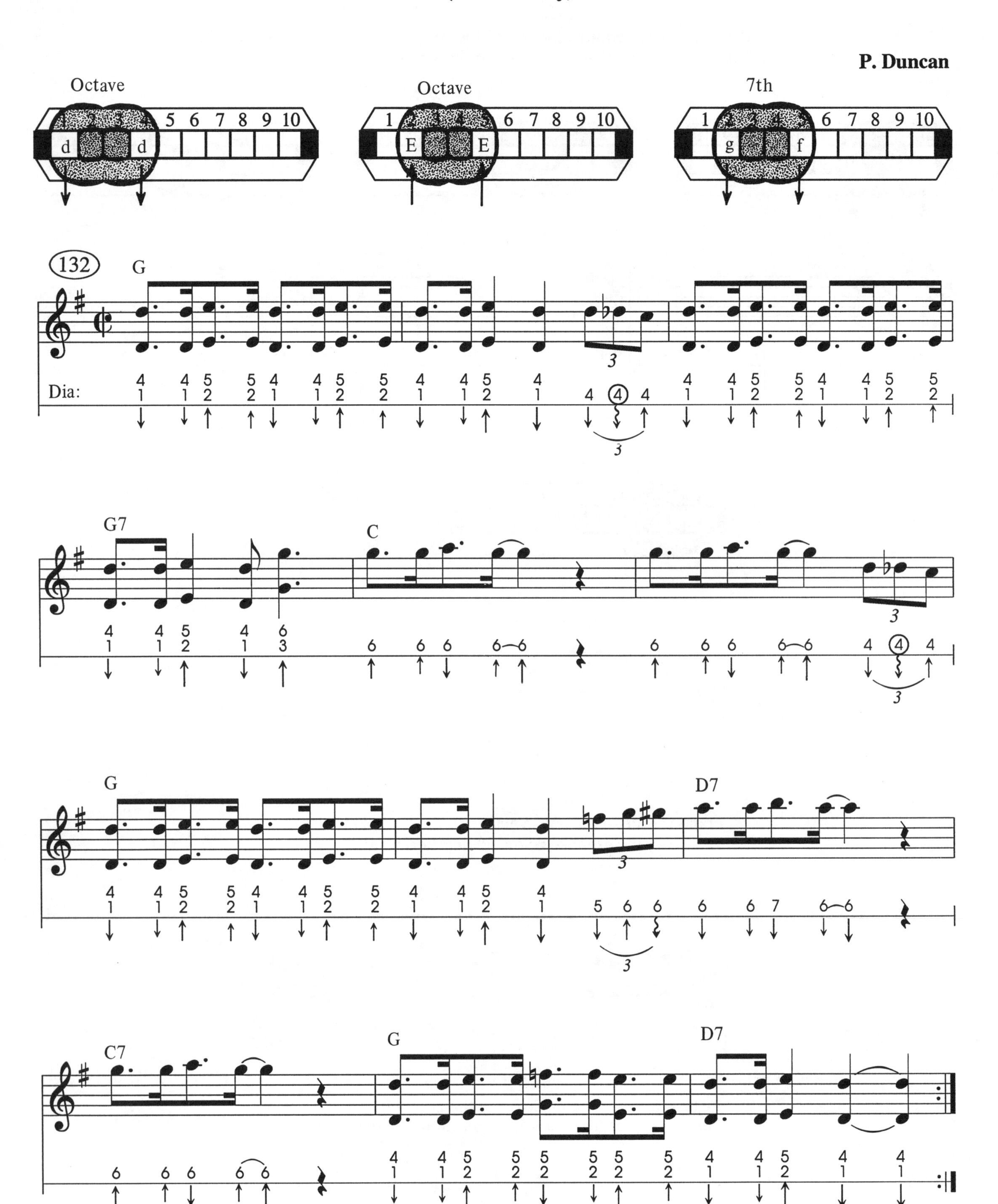

Blown
133
P. Duncan
Dia:
Flat Blue
134
P. Duncan
Dia:
Blue Bounce
135
P. Duncan
Dia:

Easy On

P. Duncan

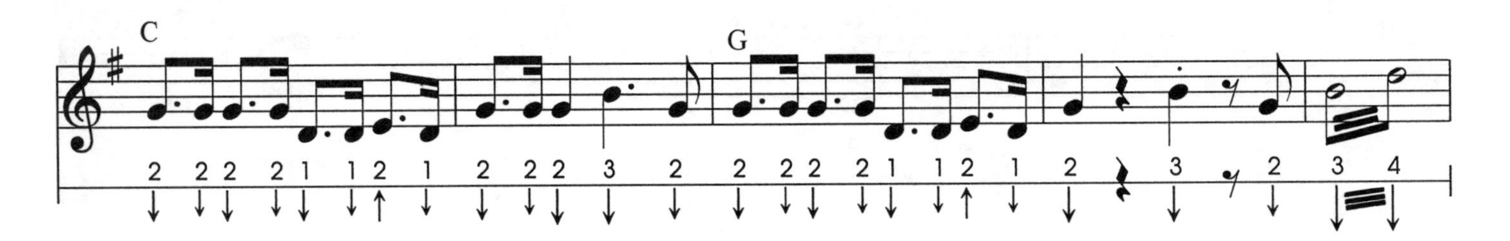

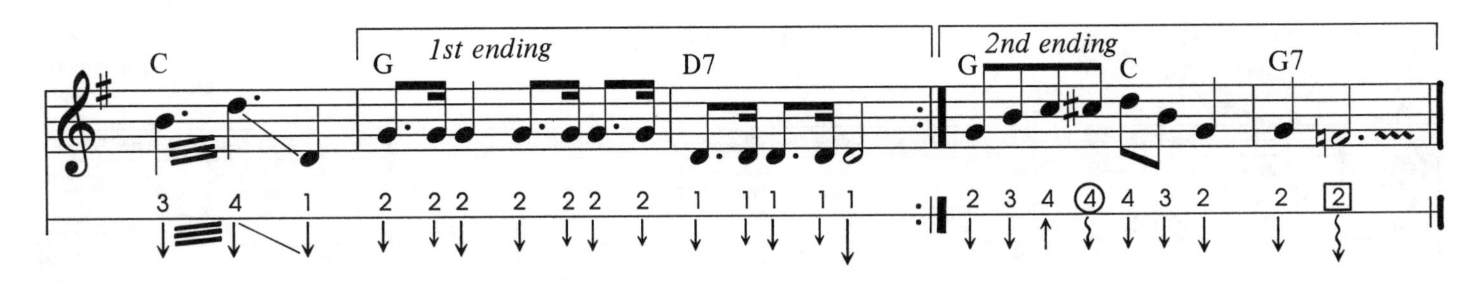

Swinging

P. Duncan

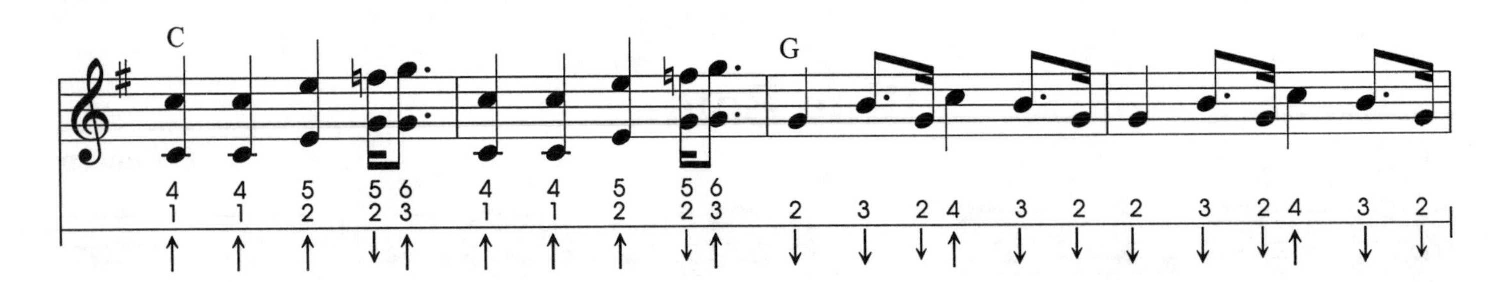

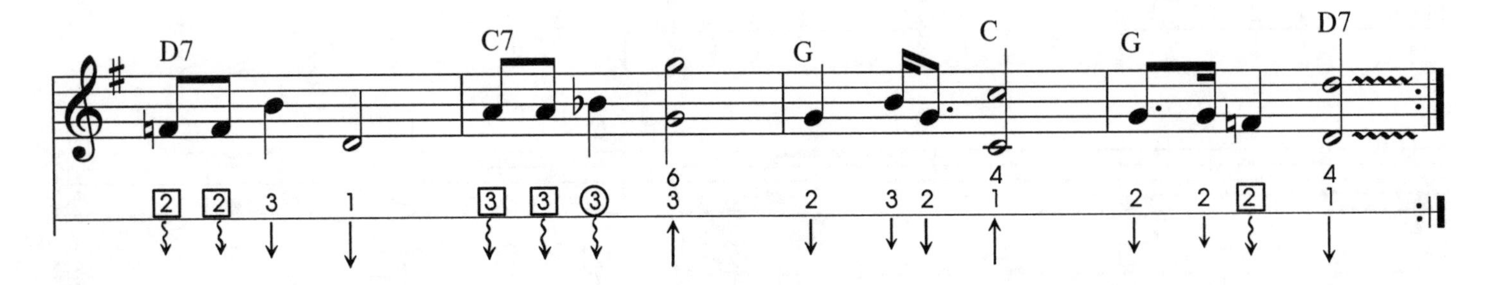

Too Natural

P. Duncan

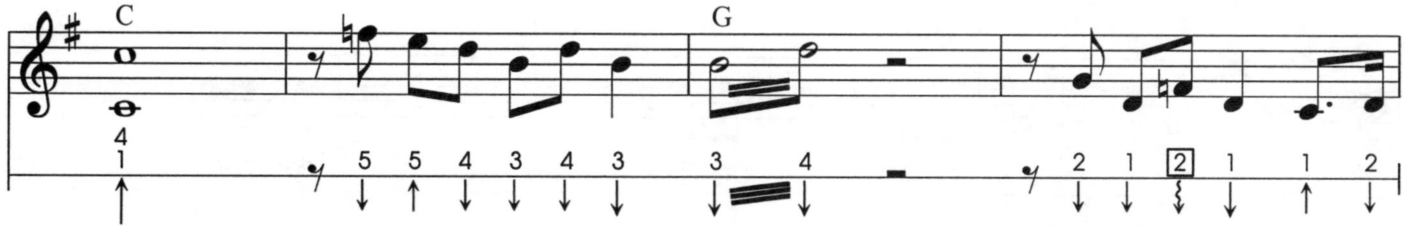

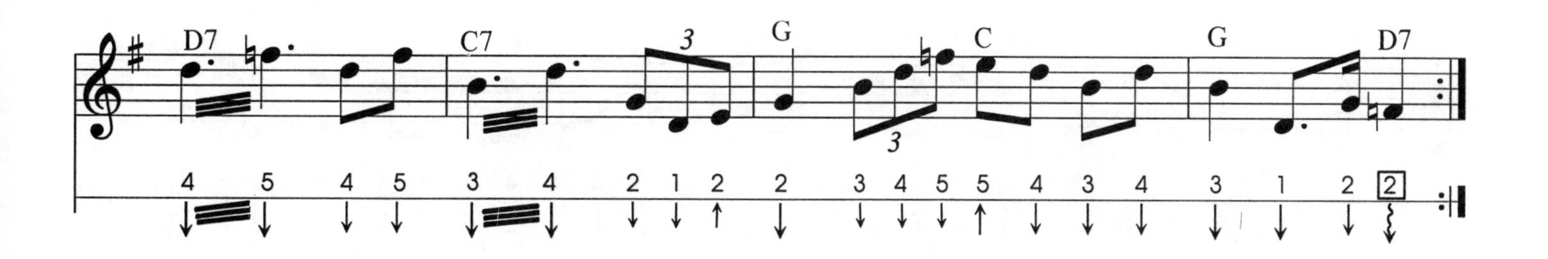

Stressed

P. Duncan

Movin'

P. Duncan

Easy Down

P. Duncan

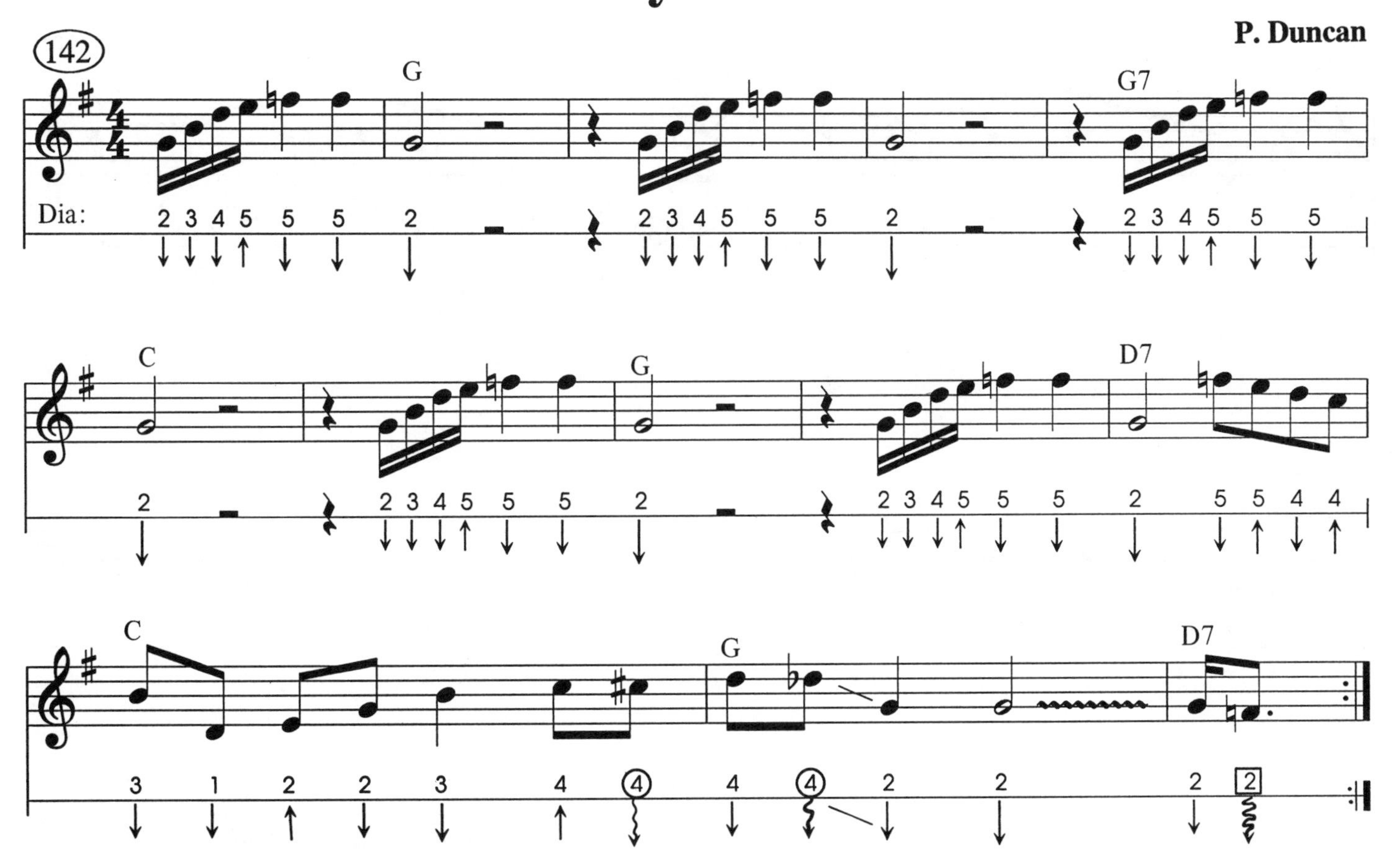

Dual Tone Vibrato*

Batting your tongue against the mouthpiece of the harmonica while drawing holes 2 and 5 will sustain pitches with a rhythm effect. Puffs of air, like throat vibrato, can do this also; but the tongue must cover holes 3 and 4.

P. Duncan

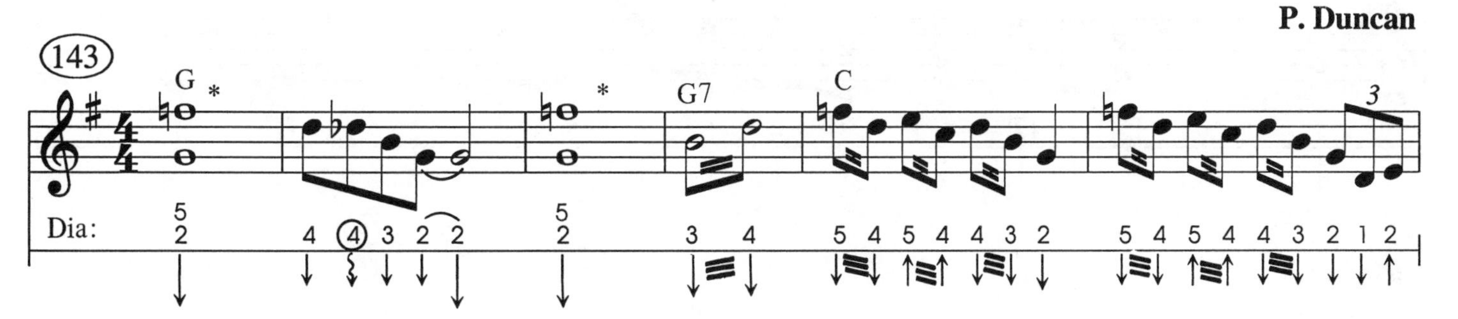

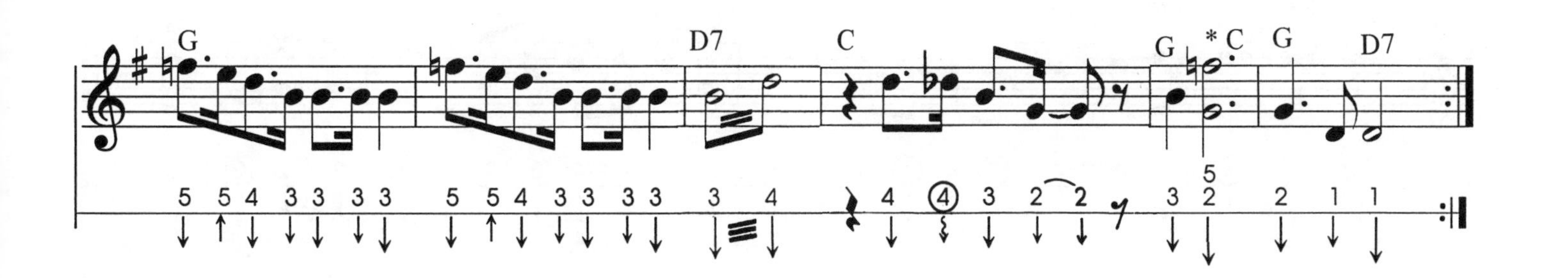

Back Down

P. Duncan

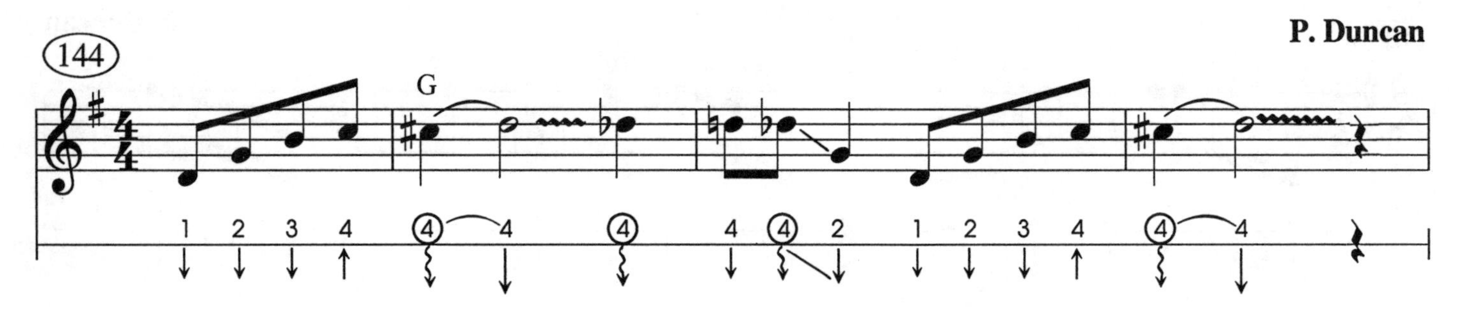

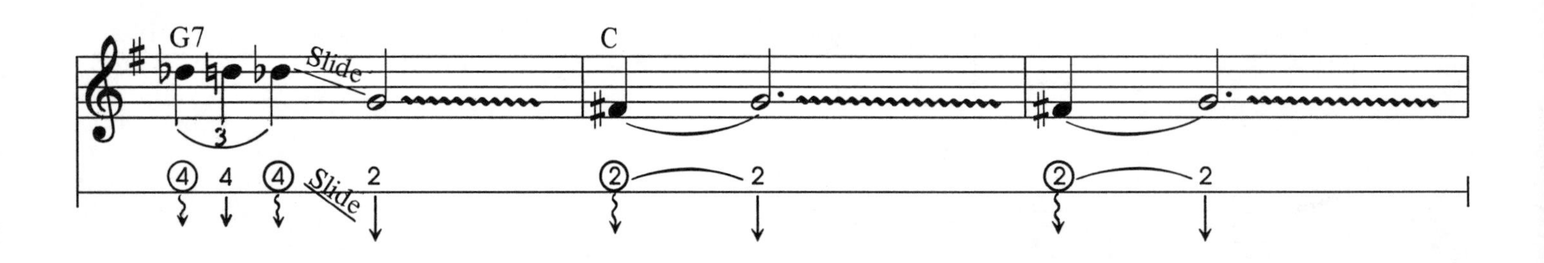

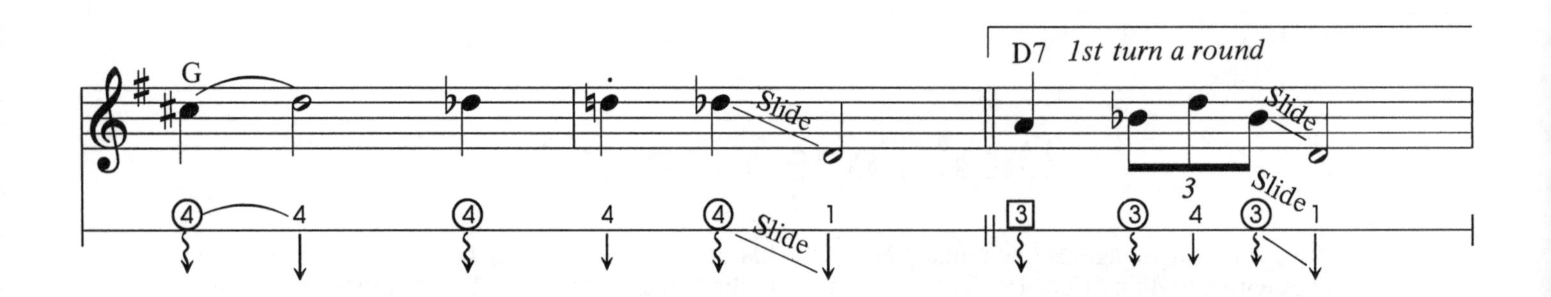

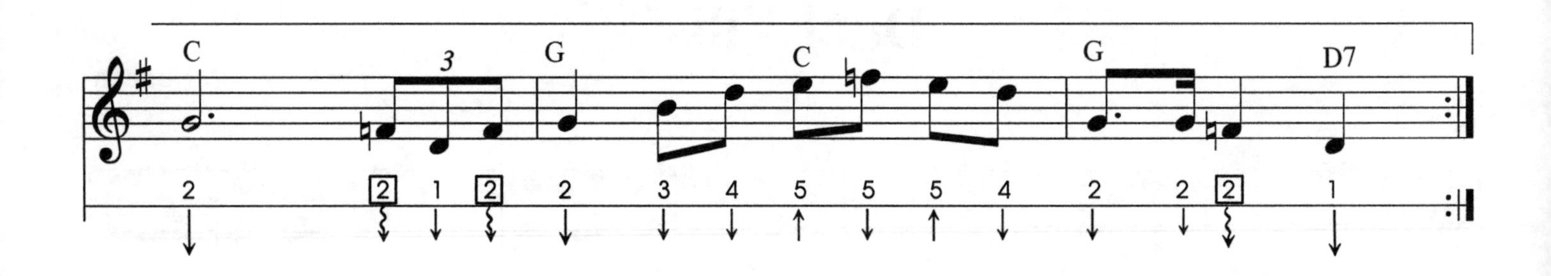

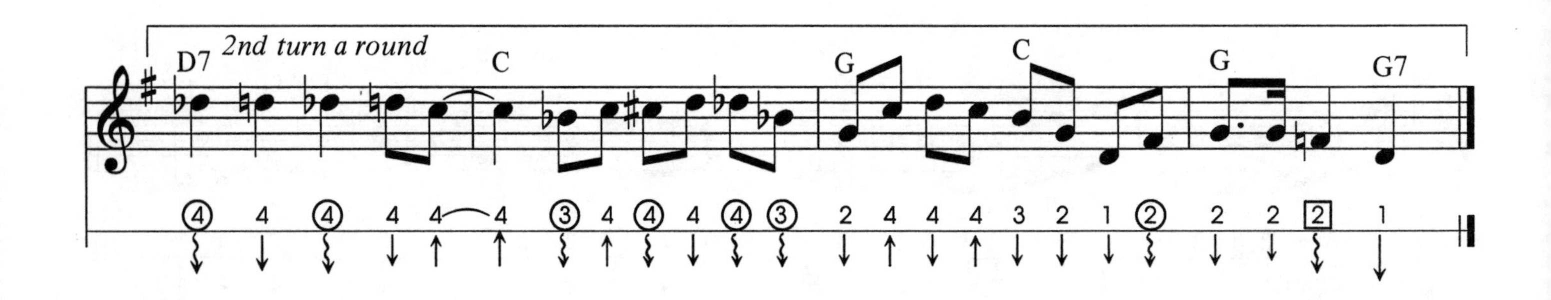

Upper Octave Blues

When we compare holes 2 through 6 with holes 6 through 9, we find the same tones but in a higher pitch.

Comparison of Scales

Ascending

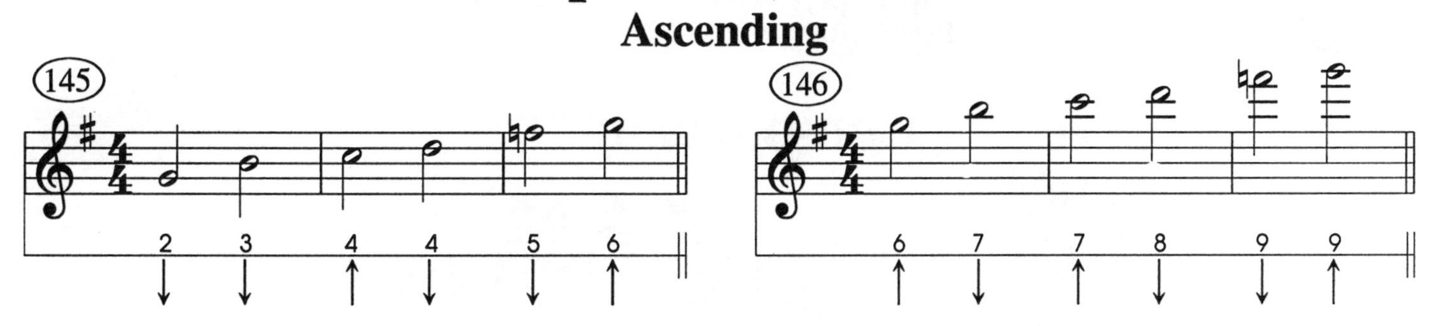

Descending

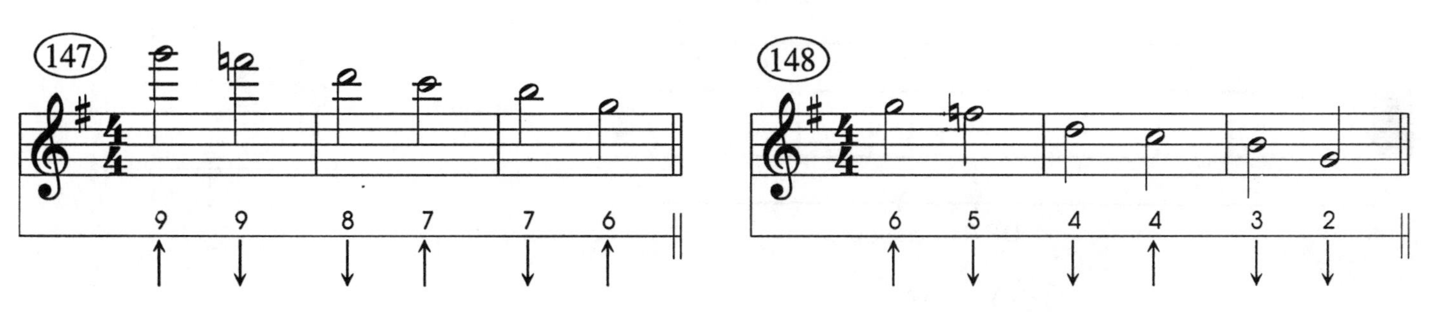

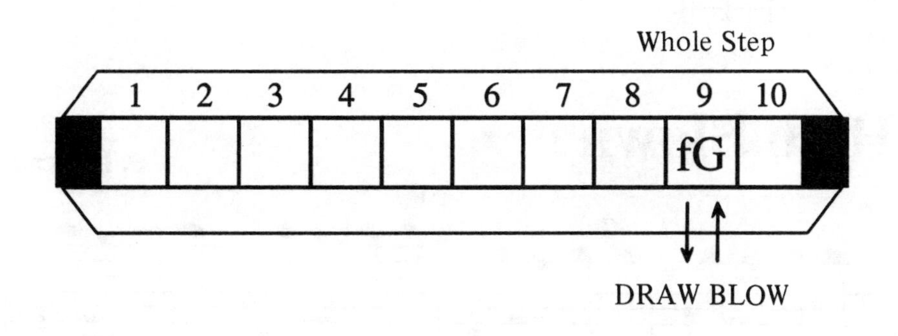

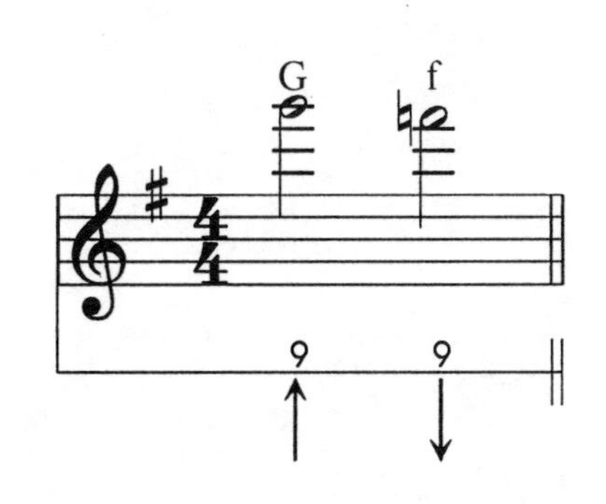

Comparison

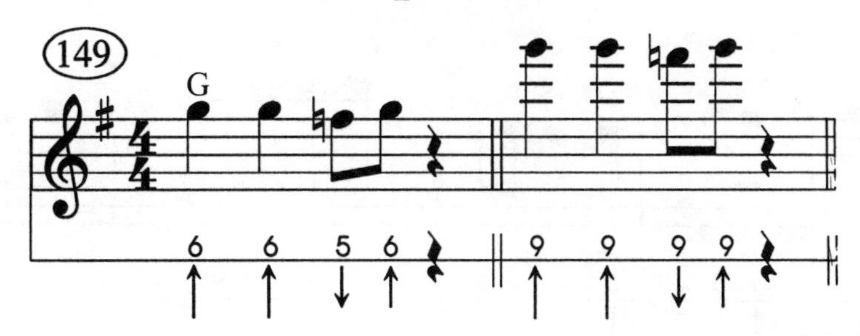

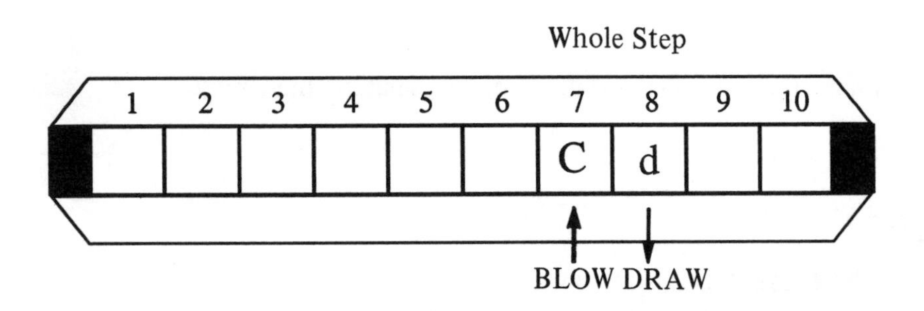

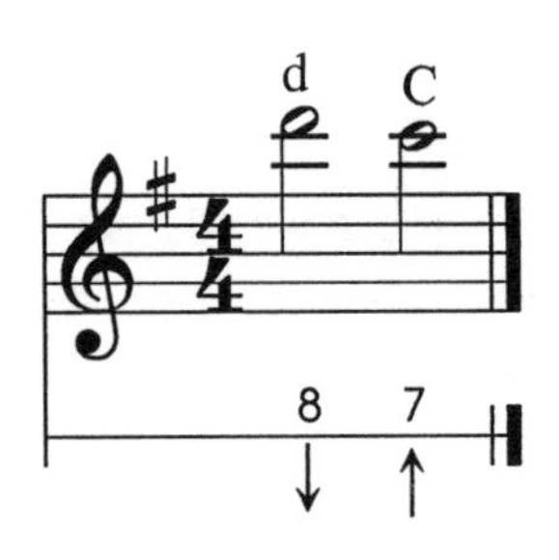

Comparison

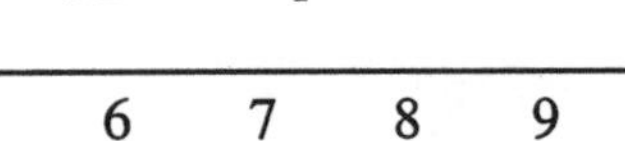

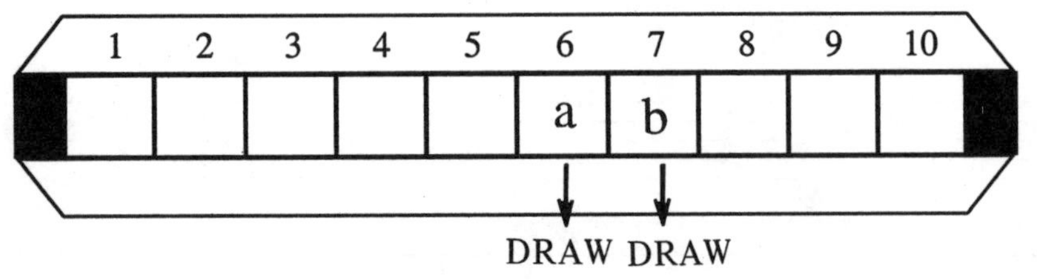

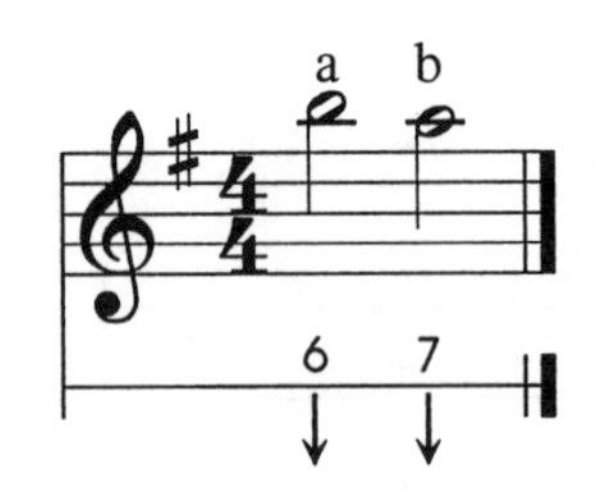

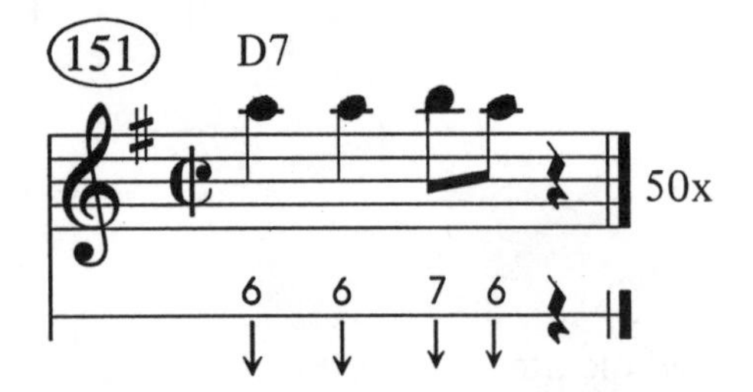

High Blown

P. Duncan

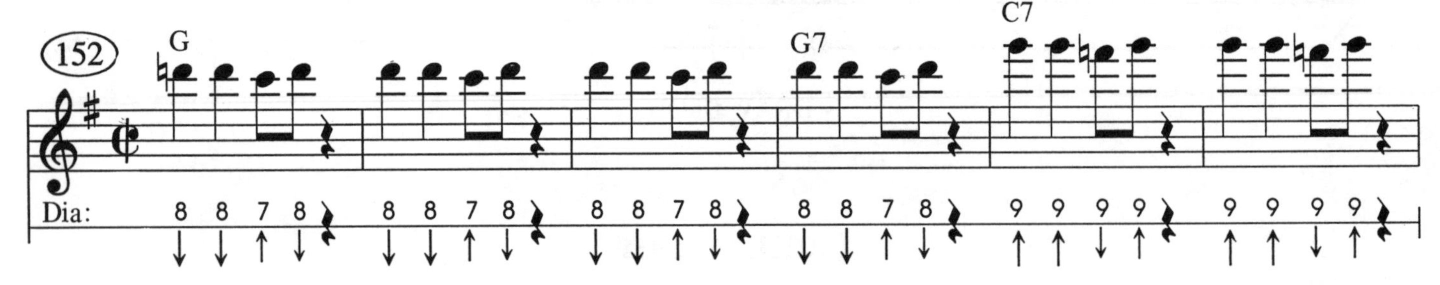

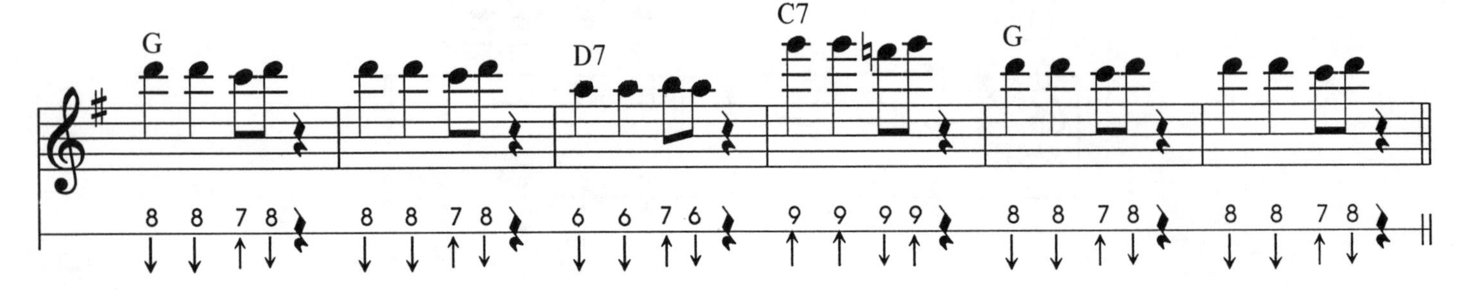

Comparison

Comparison

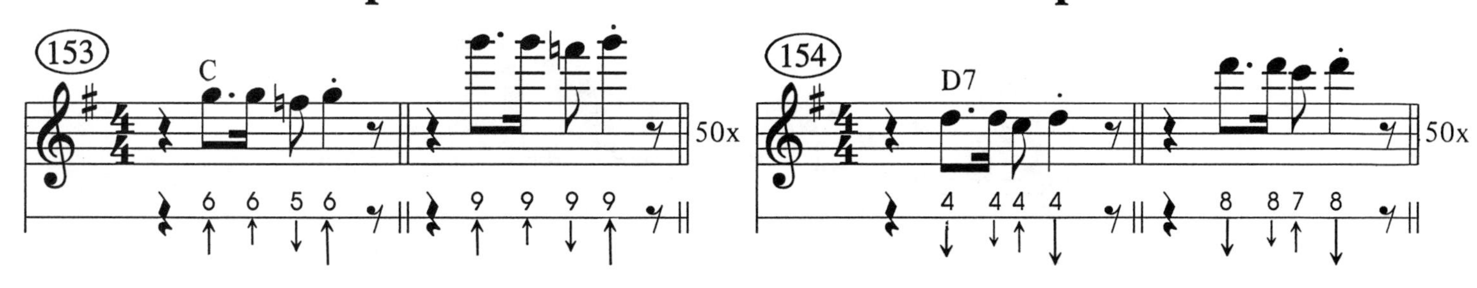

Comparison

High Blue

P. Duncan

Compare:

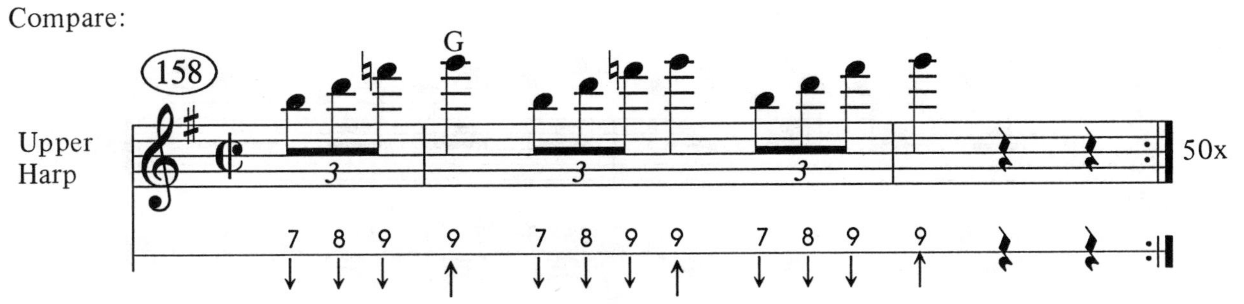

Comparison

Articulated Slide

Comparison:

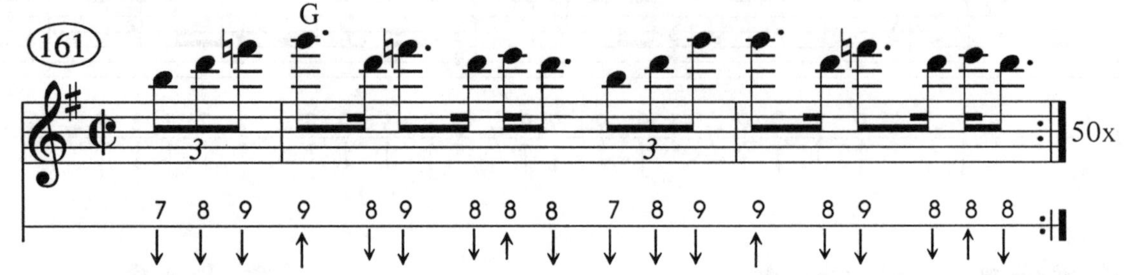

Moving Tremolo

Comparison:

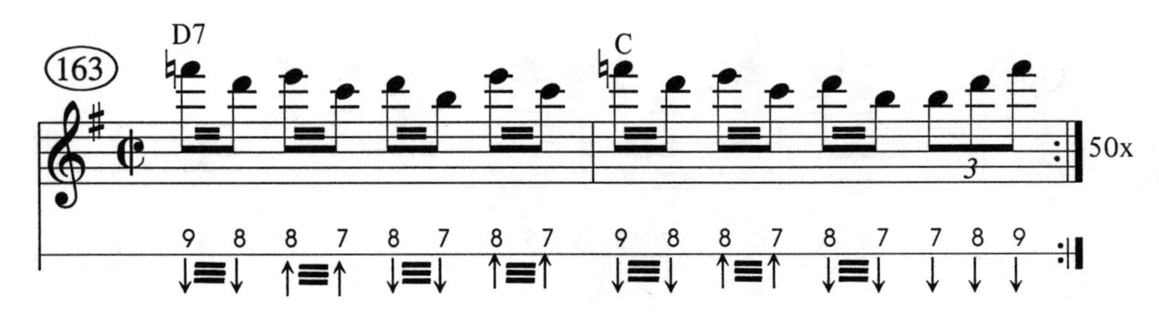

High Drive
P. Duncan
164
G
Dia:
G7
C
G
D7
C
G
D7
More Patterns
165
Middle Harp
Comparison:
166
Upper Harp
50x
Comparison
167
Middle Harp
Upper Harp
50x

Upper Blow Bend

Air Flow

Projecting air out of the mouth is the way to make the harmonica work. By changing the flow of the air and the shape of the mouth cavity, the tone can be changed to a lower pitch as you blow air. This is the way to lower or flat a tone on the harmonica, called *bending*. By changing the flow of the air (see illustration below), you can affect the pitch of the reed.

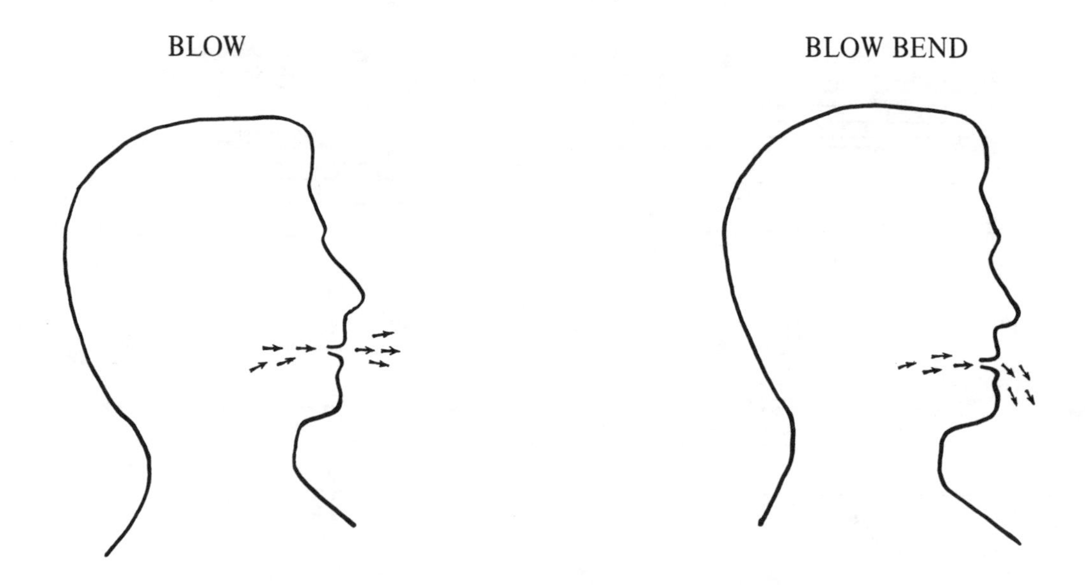

Blow Bend Hole 9

We will begin to bend blow tone "G" in hole 9. This is bent through air pressure and air direction. This works by forcing air at an angle through the chamber of the reed. The tongue rises toward the roof of the mouth, creating a smaller cavity. This increases air pressure and changes the direction of the air (see illustration).

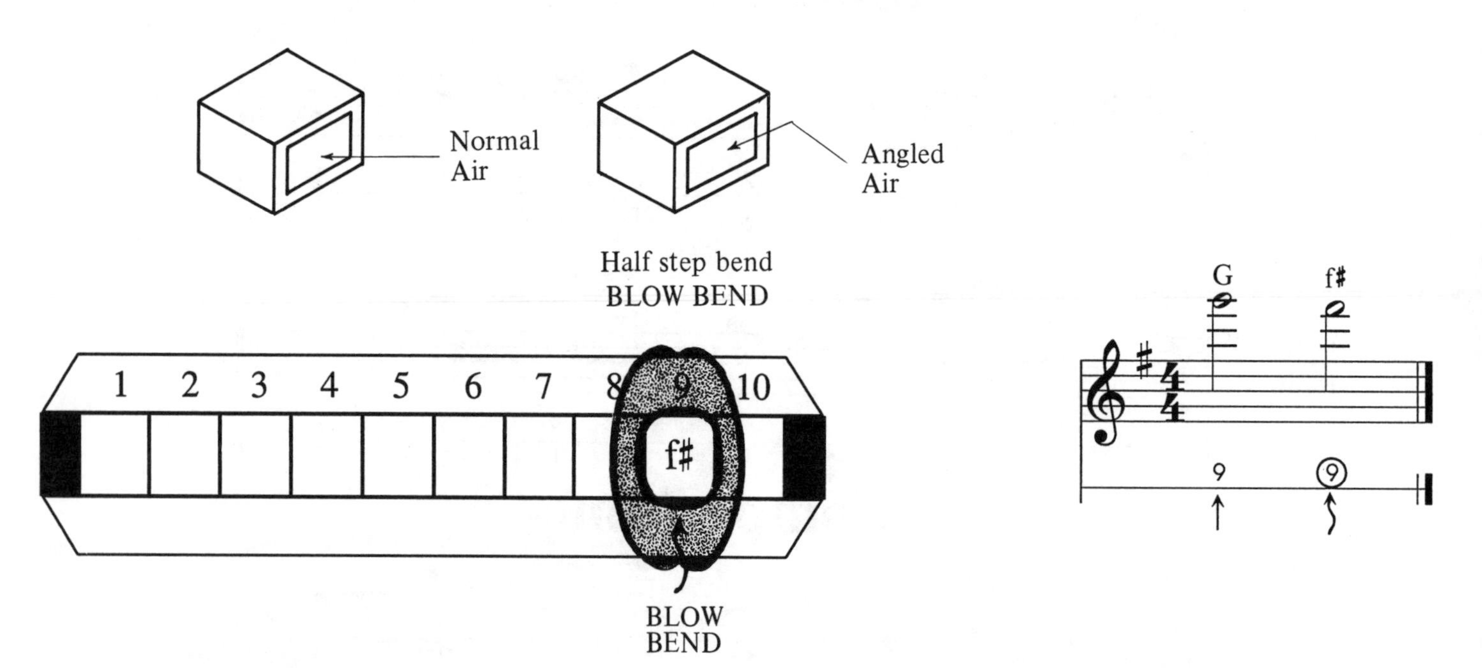

When playing hole 9 blow, a scoop or below-pitch approach ("F sharp" to "G") is sounded then allowed instantly to slide up to the actual pitch ("G"), blow hole 9.

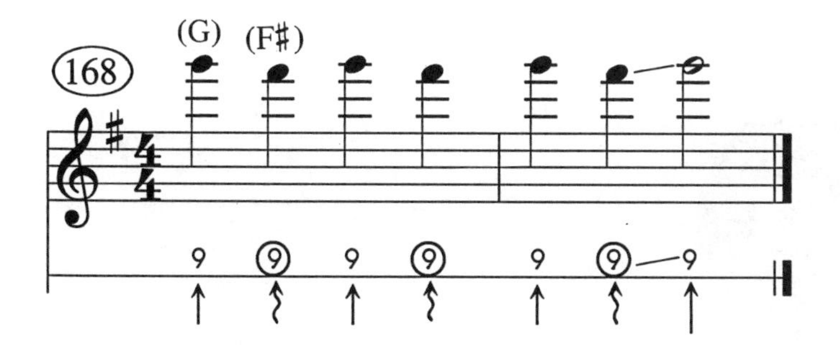

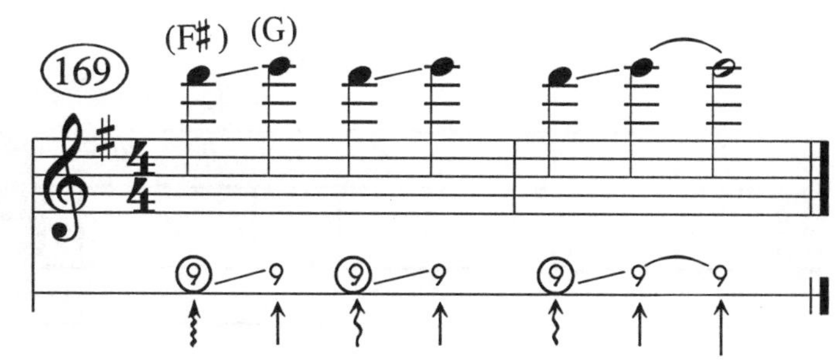

Blow Bend Hole 8

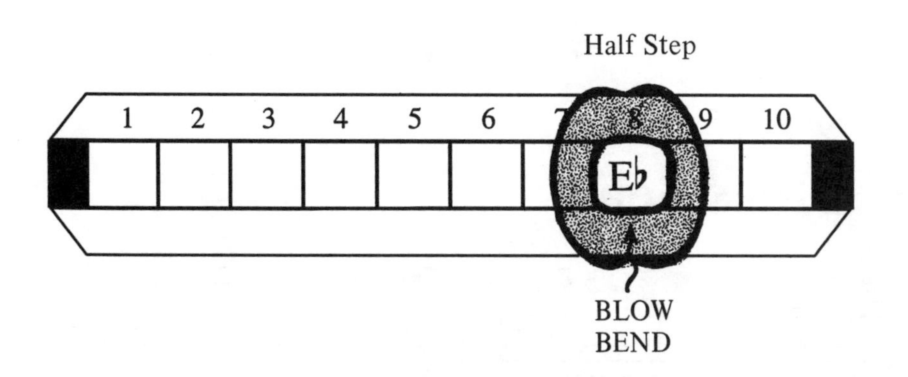

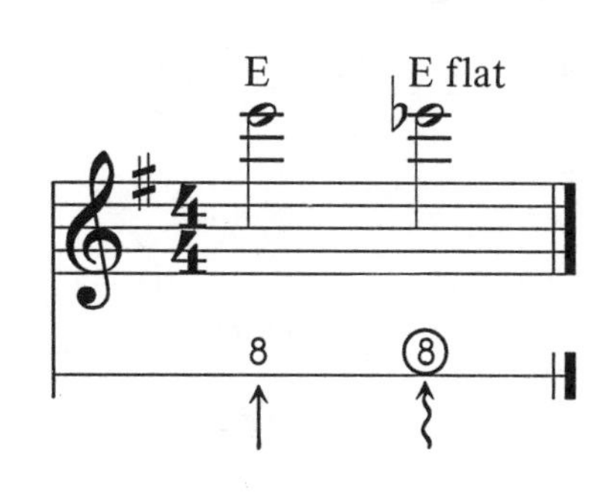

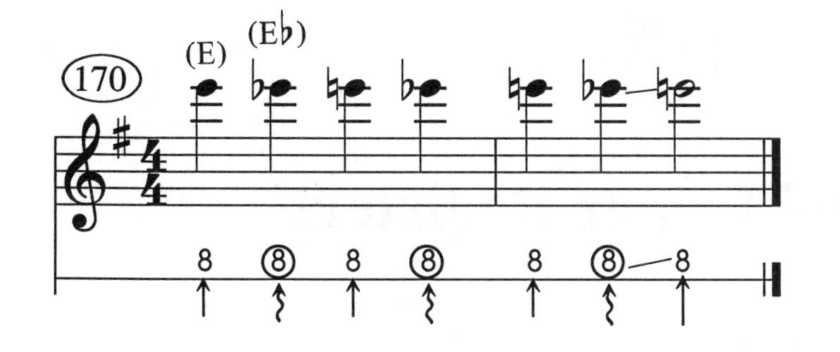

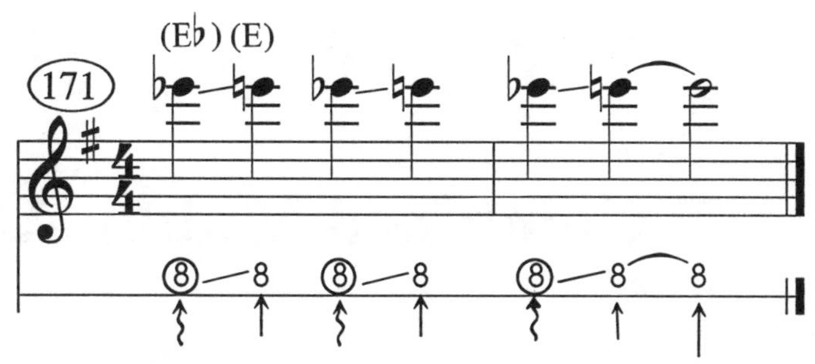

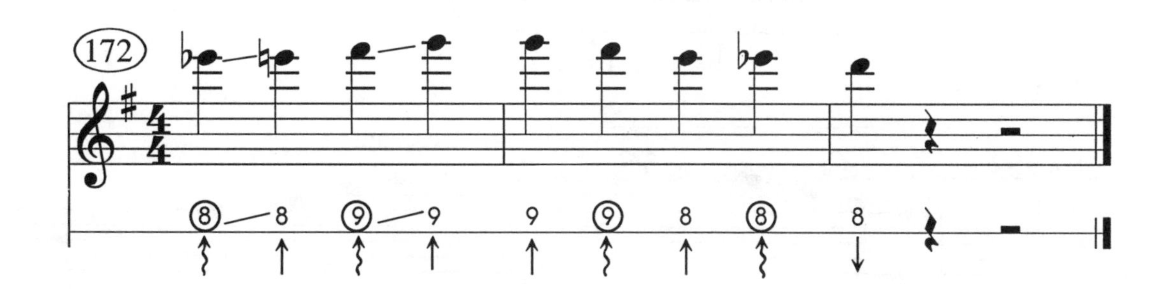

Blow Bend Hole 10

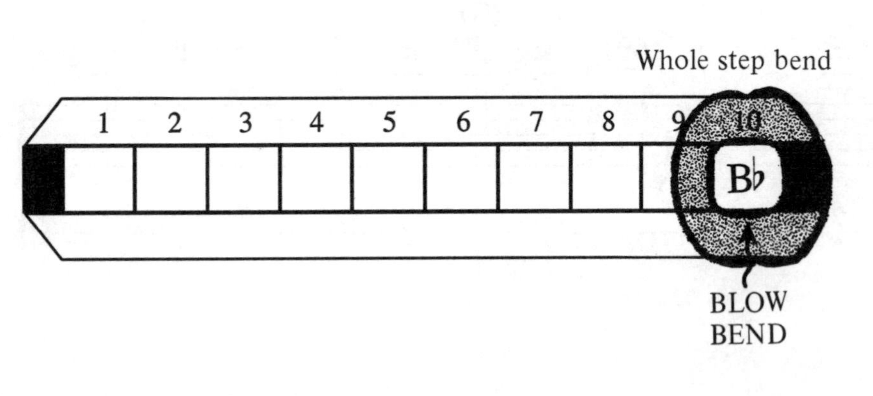

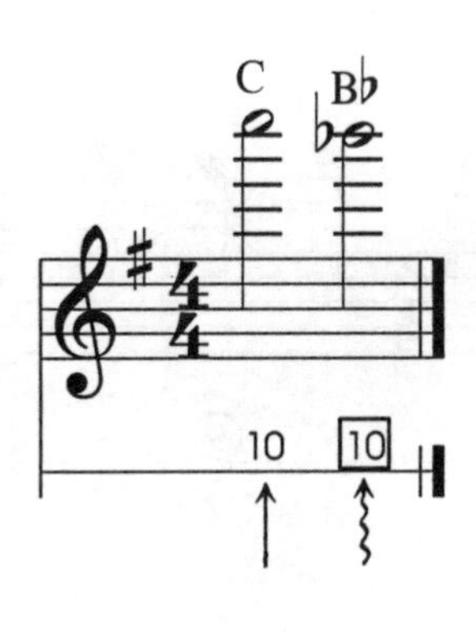

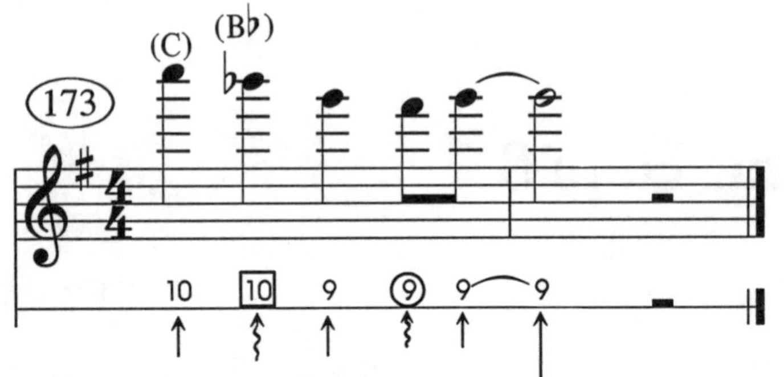

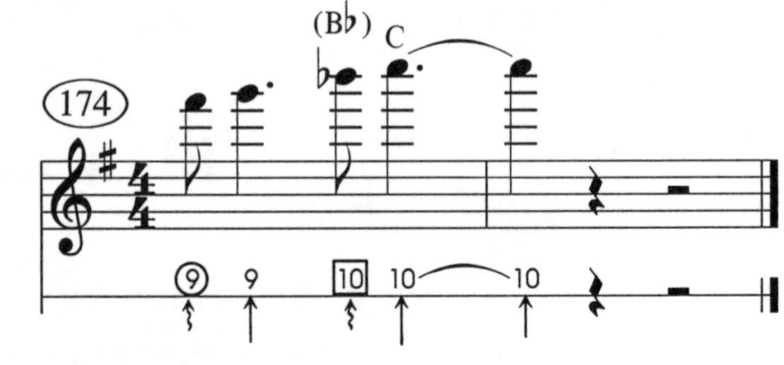

C Blues Scale

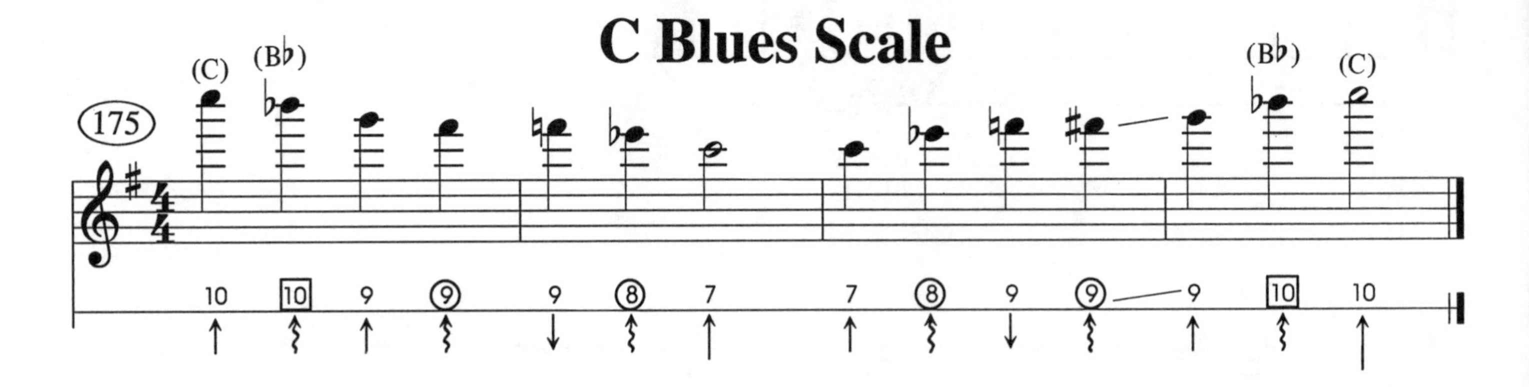

Combined Middle And Upper Registers

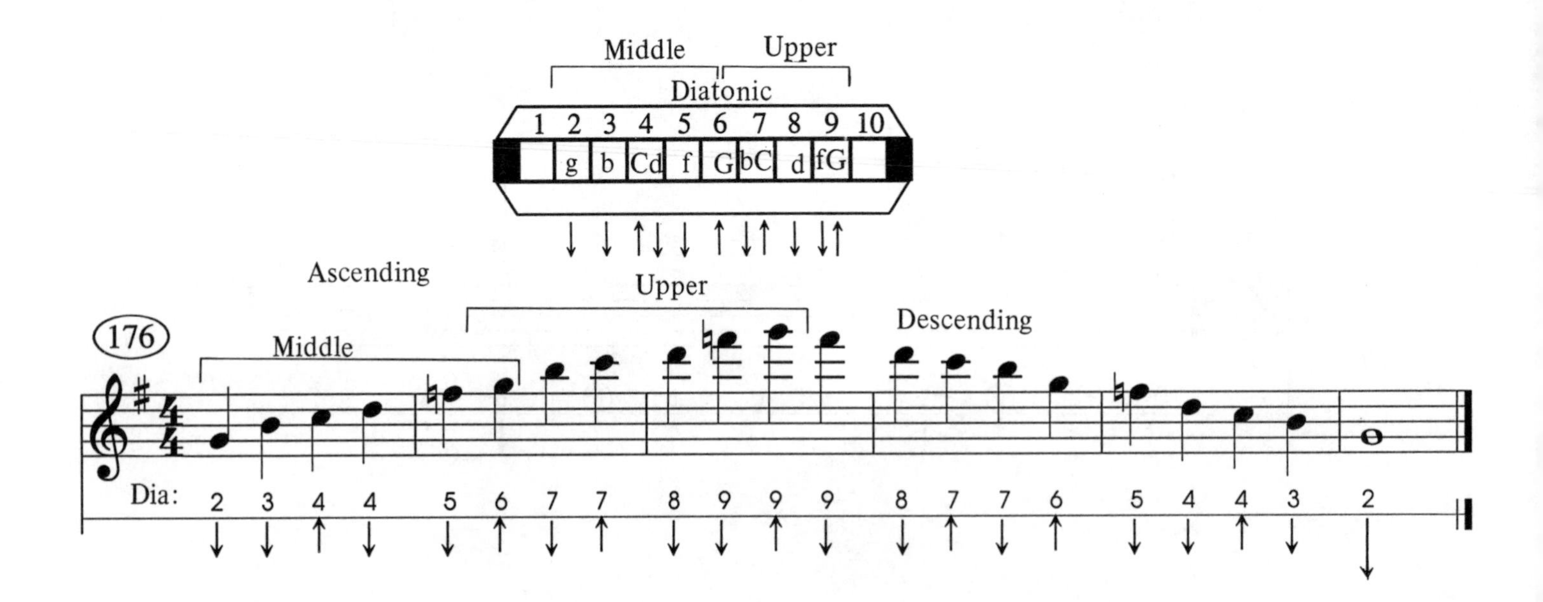

Compare Octaves

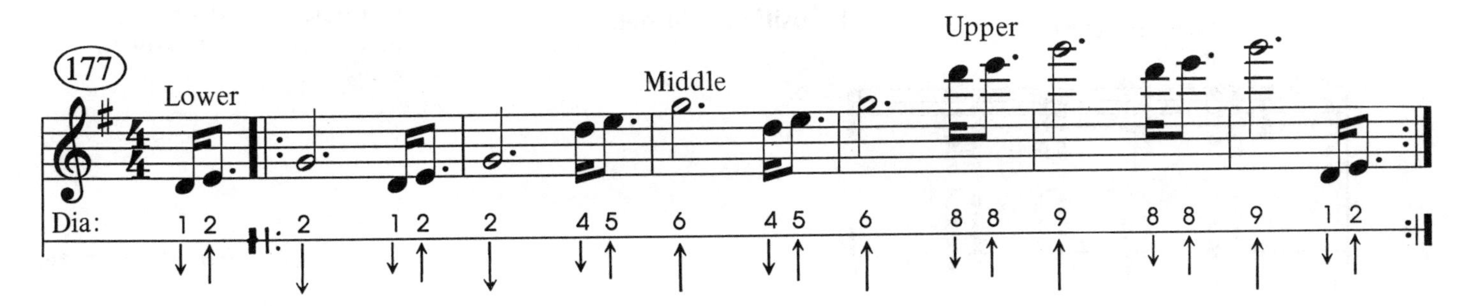

Compare and Combine

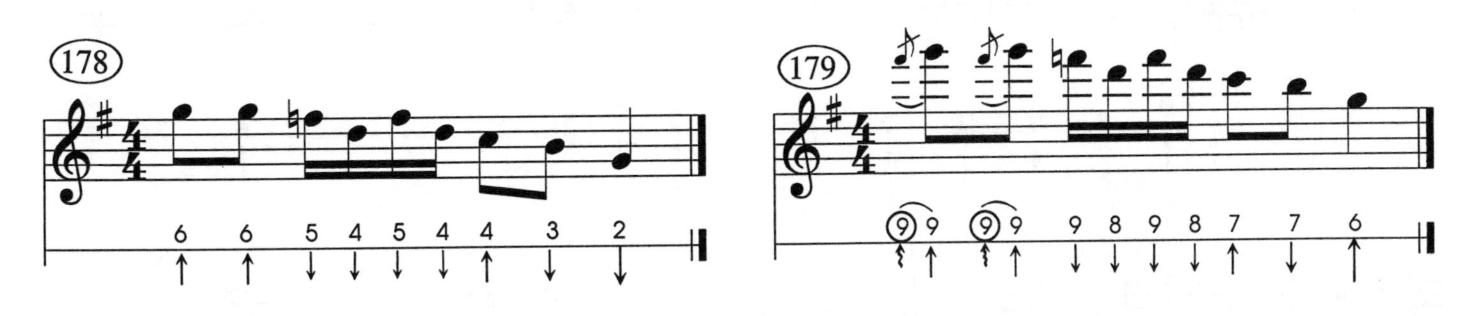

Two Octave Runs

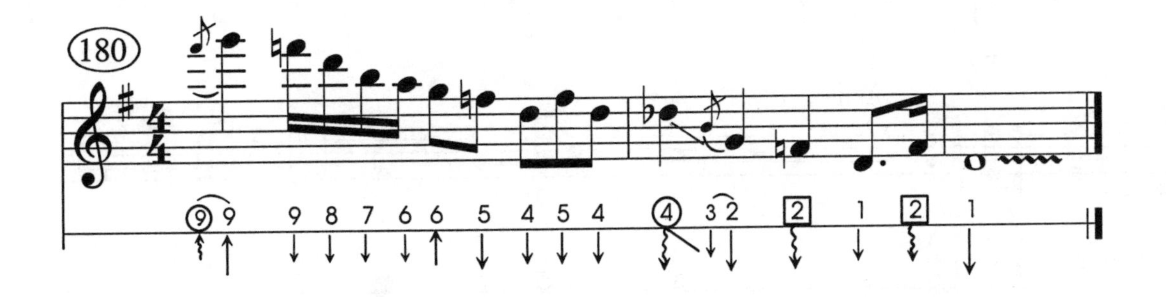

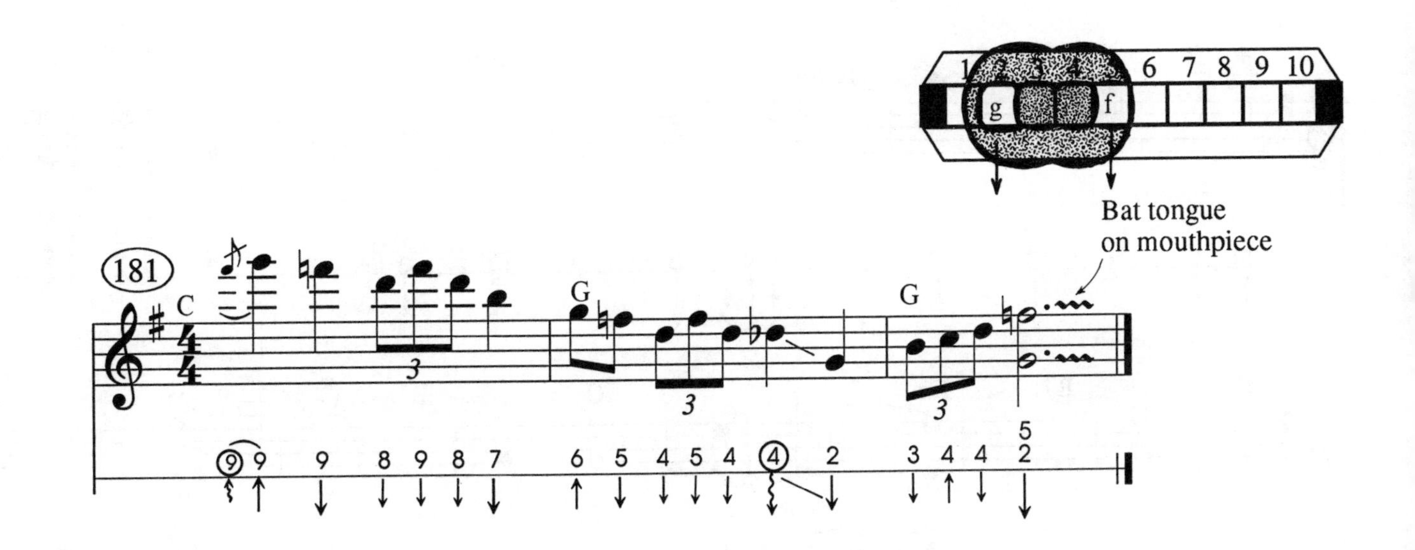

St. James

5th Position E Minor

*Hammer - on Octave: Block inner holes with the tongue immediately after the sound begins.

Hammer-On Octave:

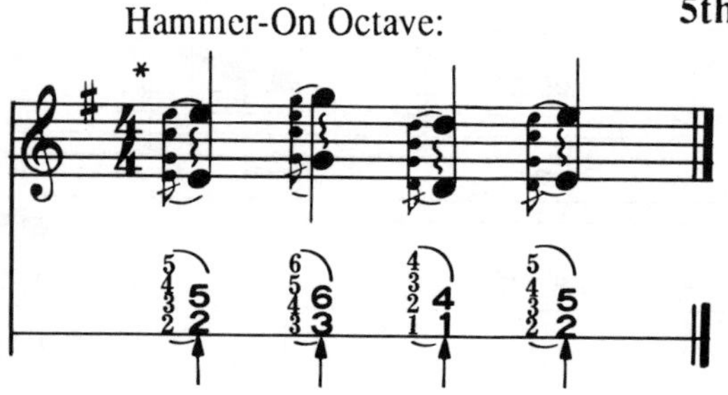

Arr. Phil Duncan

Rockin' Blues

P. Duncan

Boogie Down

P. Duncan

Hard Times
185
P. Duncan
G
Dia:
G7
C
G
Dia:
Dia:
D7
C
G
C
G
D7
G
End
Ease Up
186
P. Duncan
G
G7
C
Dia:
G
D7
C
G
D7

House Of The Rising Sun

In some cases you would play "House" in third position, that is, draw hole 4 on the diatonic 10-hole harp. This is a "sample" showing this third-position playing in D minor, starting on hole 4. Also, for accompaniment purposes, a chord chart was written for A minor, the key in which most bands play this tune. You would need a "G" diatonic harmonica and would start on draw hole 4 to play in A minor.

However, "House Of The Rising Sun" will be presented in cross-harp position, also known as second position. The "C" harmonica will play this starting on the second hole, draw. You must use bending on hole 3 at all times. G minor requires a "B flat" hole 3 slightly bent. Again, some ear training will be necessary. Use a piano or a guitar to establish the tone in your ear.

This allows for different ornamentation, that is, added improvised notes. Also, chords have been charted on the music for A minor. You would use a "D" harp in second position (starting in hole 2) cross-harp. Hole 2 is "A."

Before you play the arranged improvised version of "House Of The Rising Sun," a second presentation in G minor with no added tones is provided for rehearsal of the melody in cross-harp position. These are the actual tones for note-to-note melody.

The third presentation uses turns, slides, and runs, giving it a blues style that cross-harp position is capable of doing.

Using Different Harp Positions

1. Practice presentation #1, D minor, "C" harp.

2. Practice presentation #1, A minor, "G" harp.

3. Practice presentation #2, G minor, "C" harp.

4. Practice presentation #3, G minor, "C" harp.

5. Practice playing #3, A minor, "D" harp.

D Minor

House Of The Rising Sun

3rd Position, Draw Hole 4 "d"

Arr. P. Duncan

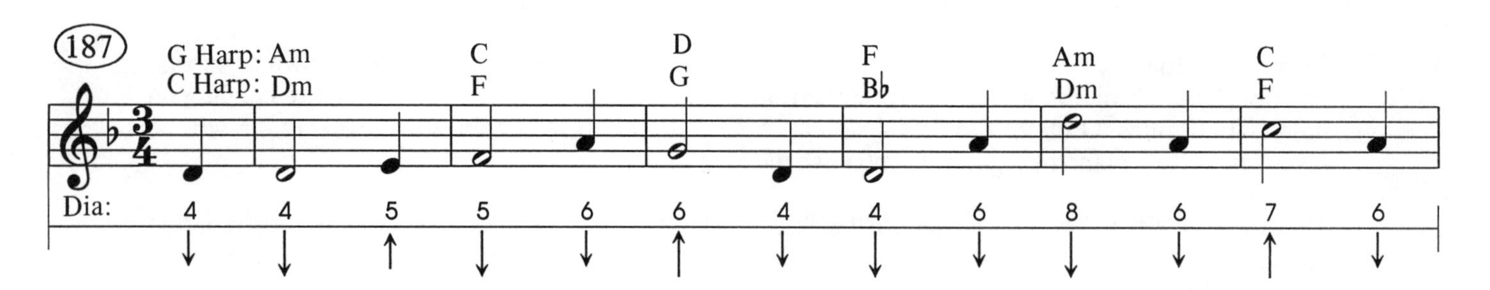

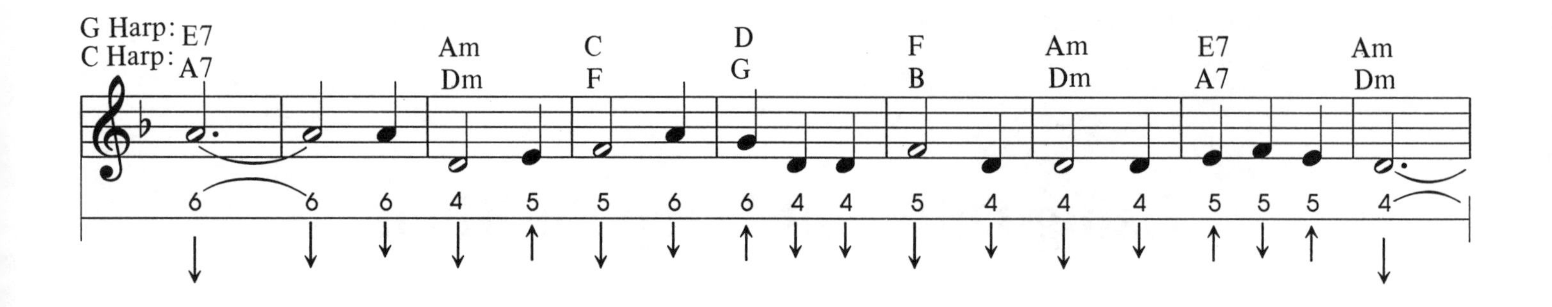

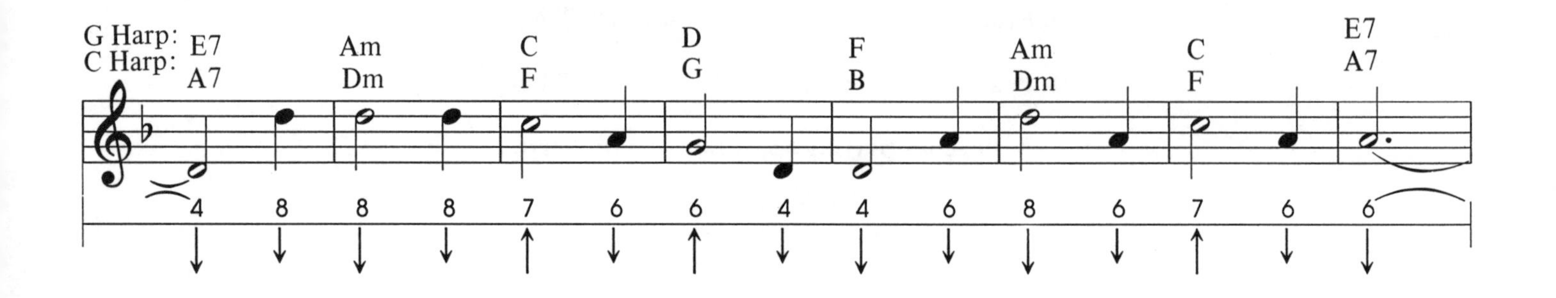

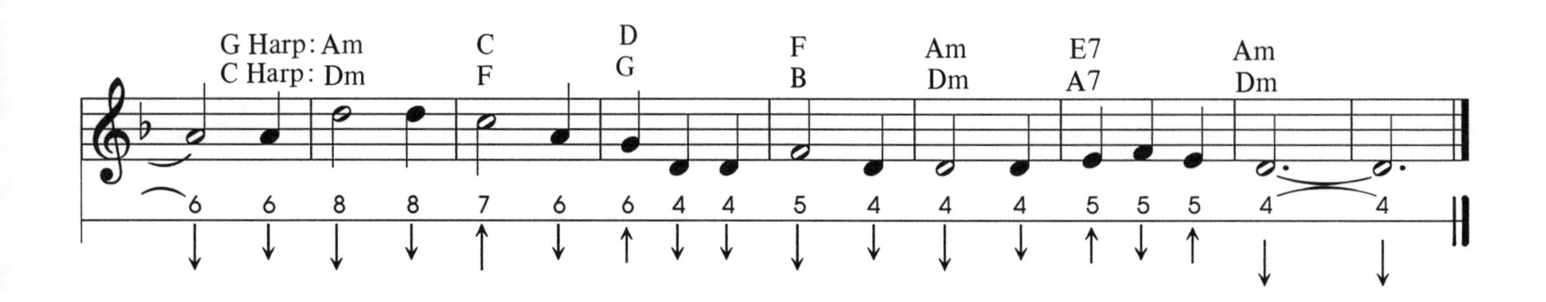

2nd Position

Cross Harp (Hole 2 Draw)

Arr. P. Duncan

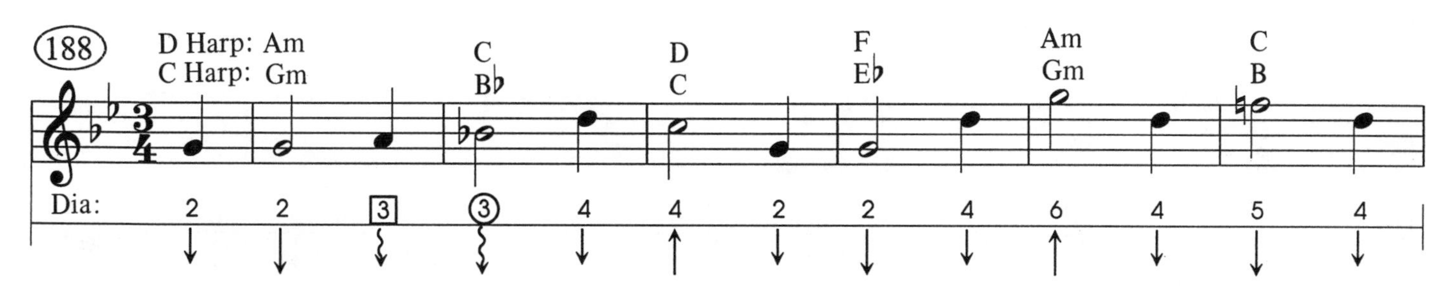

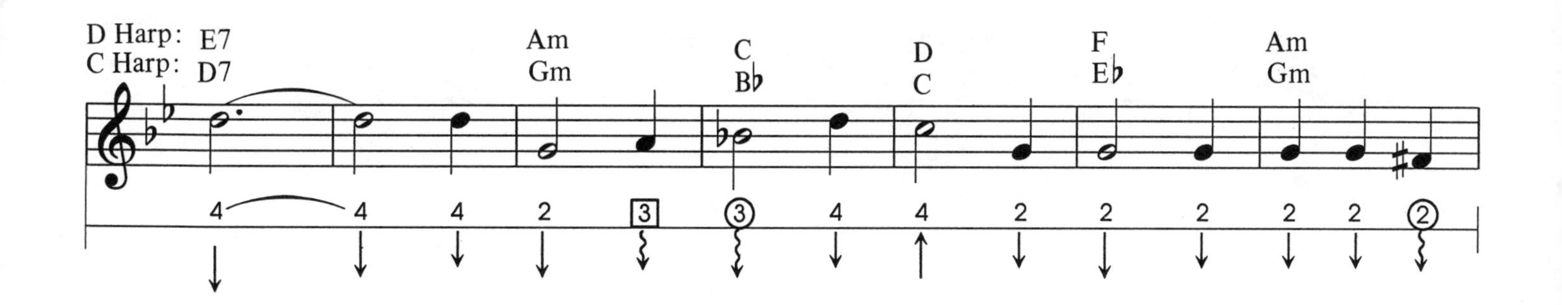

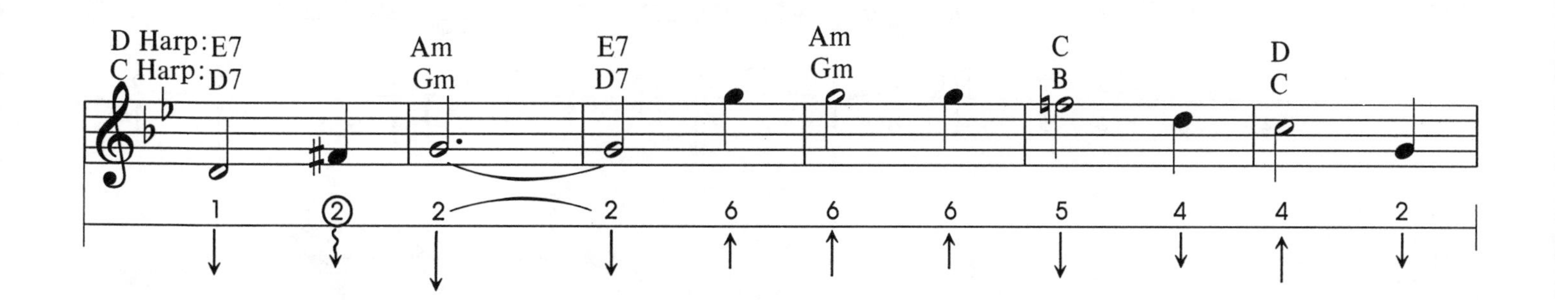

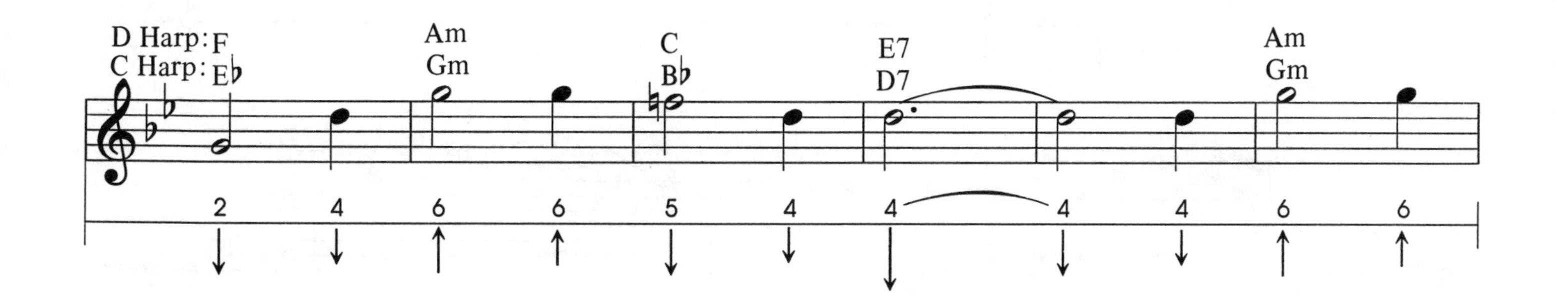

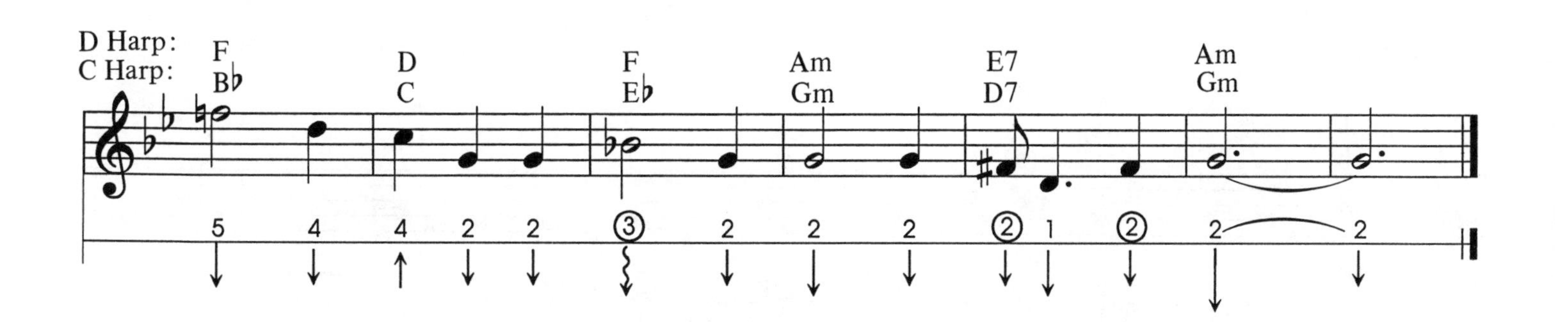

House Of The Rising Sun

2nd Position (Cross Harp)

Arr. P. Duncan

More Octave Playing

The Use Of The 64 Chromatic Harmonica

Some harp players occasionally use the chromatic harmonica to be able to play a melody using octaves (same note, eight tones apart). It is best to use a 64 chromatic harmonica for the balance and the extended left four holes. To use this technique, the mouth has to be wide open and the tongue must cover three holes at the same time. At first this is very uncomfortable, but as you practice it will become tolerable.

You will need to use your ears to hear the "same pitch." Remember to put more harmonica into your mouth and spread your tongue over three middle holes. Blow and draw air through the corners of your mouth.

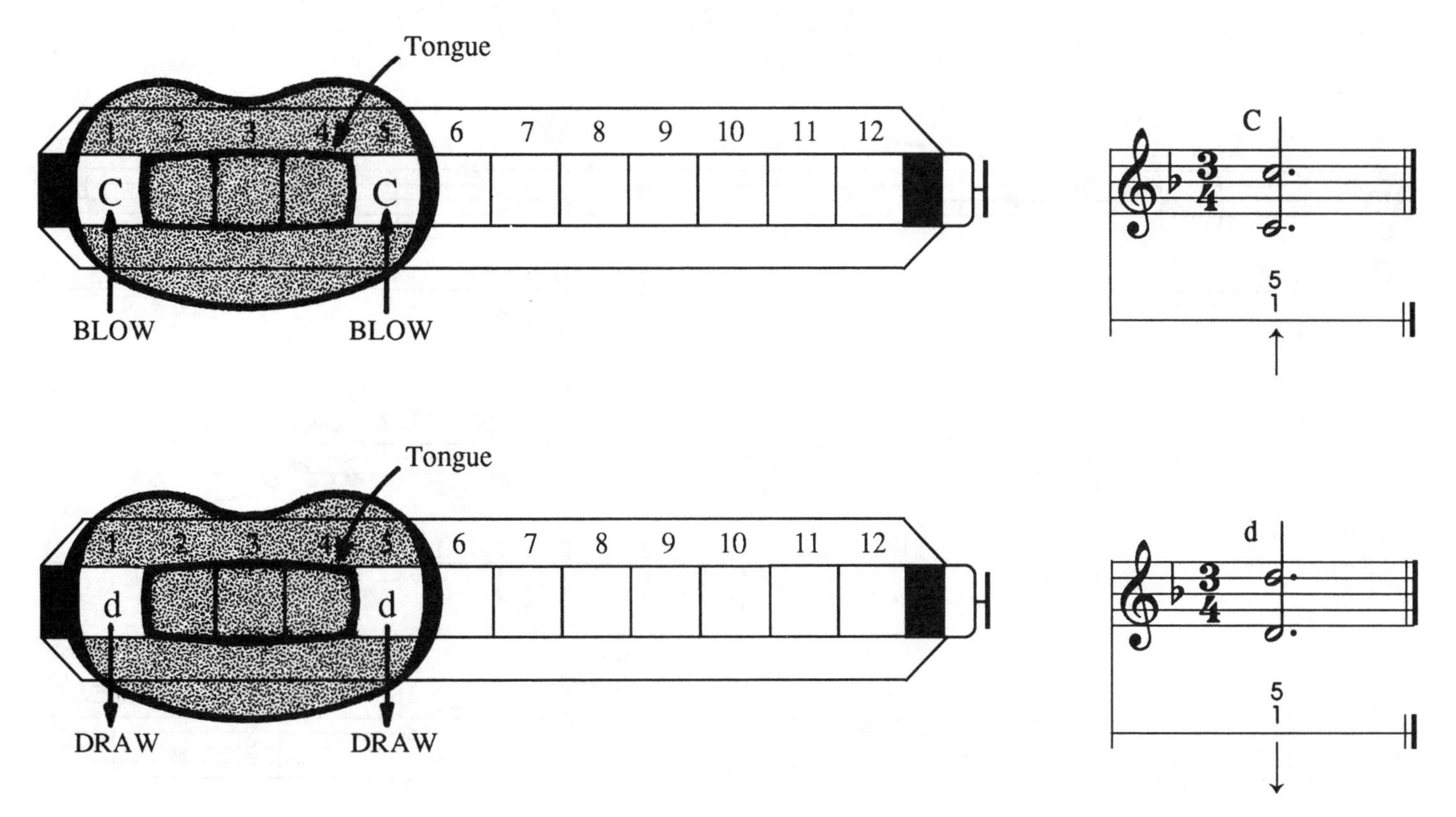

Tip: This technique will improve your diatonic 10-hole harp octave playing.

"Scarborough Fair" is arranged to be played using single tones, then octave pitches, then repeat the single-tone portion. This makes a good contrast for the melody and a nice way to play a slow waltz-style of music. It is also a contrast to the standard blues style.

This chromatic harp is played in third position, that is, we start on hole 1 or 5, draw. This sets up a D minor-type of scale. Playing other tunes in this minor, you can use this technique to produce excellent harmonica sounds and arrangements.

You use different keys for two reasons, either to get a high-sound melody or a lower one; but mostly you would change keys (harmonicas) to fit your voice range.

Third Position Draw Hole 5

Scarborough Fair

Chromatic

(190)

Arr. P. Duncan